EMBRAC
ALIENATION

EMBRACING ALIENATION

Why We Shouldn't Try to Find Ourselves

Todd McGowan

Published by Repeater Books

An imprint of Watkins Media Ltd

Unit 11 Shepperton House

89-93 Shepperton Road

London

N1 3DF

United Kingdom

www.repeaterbooks.com

A Repeater Books paperback original 2024

1

Distributed in the United States by Random House, Inc., New York.

Copyright © Todd McGowan 2024

Todd McGowan asserts the moral right to be identified as the author of this work.

ISBN: 9781915672223

Ebook ISBN: 9781915672230

Printed and bound in the UK by TJ Books

Contents

For Jane and Del Neroni,
who both found freedom in alienation.

Introduction
What Is to Be Left Undone?

Alienation sounds unappealing. The term itself creates the impression of a disruptive process that we should find a way to avoid. No one has ever said to their friends, "Let's all go get alienated." Alienation seems to have nothing in common with pleasant activities like forming a community, embarking on a romance, hanging out with friends, eating pizza, playing tennis, or getting drunk. These are things that people take up eagerly, in contrast to alienation. Even in everyday parlance, we treat alienation as a lamentable condition that we should try to avoid. We want to help the teenager escape it or lead the alienated outsider toward feeling more integrated. Theoretically, following the thinking of Karl Marx, leftists imagine political activity as a fight against alienation. From almost every perspective, people view alienation as a problem to be surmounted.

But this verdict on alienation misses its emancipatory quality. Alienation has historically gotten a bad rap. We should think of alienation much more positively than we do. We should think of it as the basis for our capacity for transcending whatever our given situation might be. We should sit around extolling the virtues of alienation and trying to find ways to heighten our experience of it.

Although no one has explicitly championed alienation as a project, there are lines of thinking that point toward alienation as the basis for emancipation. German Idealism, culminating in the philosophy of Hegel, views alienation as the condition for any self-awareness. Psychoanalysis, for its part, grasps the alienation of the subject as the irreducible fact of our existence and works to reconcile people with it. In a related way, the existentialism of Jean-Paul Sartre and Simone de Beauvoir sees the subject's alienation as the basis for freedom. Frantz Fanon brings together all these currents — Hegel, psychoanalysis, and existentialism — to formulate an anticolonial theory critical of efforts to avoid confronting our fundamental alienation. That said, for these thinkers, alienation never becomes the explicit watchword of their project. And yet, it is what unites these disparate attempts to think through how we should conceive emancipation. This project will being alienation to the fore and argue on its behalf.

The paradox of alienation is that it doesn't mark a deviation from an original identity that we once had and lost but constitutes who we are. Alienation occurs, but it doesn't alienate us from what we once really were. Instead, alienation is primary. We are alienated in our subjectivity, and alienation persists until our death. Death is the only possible cure for it, which is one reason why we probably shouldn't try so hard to overcome it.[1] Far from being something to rue or to escape, the fact of alienation is the condition of possibility for what makes our existence worth enduring — freedom, equality, solidarity, and our capacity for transcending our situation.

All creation depends on alienation, which is a process that uproots us from our place and from the given properties of our existence. As it dislocates us, alienation frees us from our situation. Even though all people are born into a specific social situation in which powerful forces act on them, they are not reducible to the place where they emerge or to these determinative forces, no matter how powerful they may be. As a result of the primary alienation in language, an internal distance forms that allows people to relate to themselves as if to another entity, at the same time as it distances them from others who surround them. We are alienated both from ourselves and from others. No matter what we do, we will never overcome this alienation. It is the basic fact of our existence.

Alienation is the lack of self-identity. This lack of self-identity gives the subject distance from the conditions out of which it emerges. If I am not identical to myself, if I am at odds with myself, I cannot be completely determined by external forces. As a being separated from myself that is not just one thing, I can never just be what any external forces would have me be. My internal split indicates a resistance to what my biology or my society would make me. Explicit distance from itself gives subjectivity an ability to act against what would otherwise determine it. Social and natural determinations can lose their decisive grip on the subject because its alienation from itself can render these determinations insignificant.

Rather than just living out my existence as a creature of a small Midwestern American town, I have the ability to leave and become someone who challenges the determinants of this situation because I am never identical with the position into which I am born. This gives me the possibility of relating to this position critically, so much so that I might decide to abandon all the ideas and the values that this community hands down to me. Raised to be an enthusiastic capitalist subject, I might become a Marxist one. Pressured to be masculine, I might become feminine. Determined to love the American Midwest, I might decide to work in Argentina. And so on. The failure to be exactly what one is — one's being out

3

of joint — is what makes a break from one's original situation possible. But even if I remain within this situation and accept its judgments, I nonetheless relate to them as if they were alien to me. One doesn't have to leave home to be an alien there. Just like everyone, I have an internal foreignness that interrupts the transmission of the community's dictates to me.

Without this internal distance, one could not emerge as a subject with the ability to relate to itself. An initial split generates and defines subjectivity. Our separation from ourselves enables us to be who we are by emphasizing that we are inextricable from what is foreign within us.[2] The foreignness within is essential to who we are. It gives us our singularity.

This internal foreignness is what Sigmund Freud calls the unconscious.[3] The existence of the unconscious places a barrier between the subject and its situation as well as between the subject and itself. Only alienated beings have an unconscious, but the alien status of the unconscious implies that the unconscious actually has us. We don't have it. This internal foreigner dictates how the subject acts, where it directs its concern, and what it finds compelling. The unconscious orients subjectivity as it expresses subjectivity's self-division.[4]

The unconscious drives subjects to act against their self-interest, thus making evident their alienation from themselves. Instead of eating apples and broccoli to prevent coronary disease, someone might binge on doughnuts and cupcakes. Rather than choosing a compatible romantic partner, someone else opts for a person who produces nothing but painful clashes. Another person continues to seek out intoxicants despite knowing the dangers that they pose to a long and healthy life. Someone else constantly ends up on the wrong side of the boss at work while professing a wish for professional advancement. In each case, self-destructive actions take place that evade the person's conscious control.

Everyone exists with an internal force that constantly undermines their conscious wishes. When people act in ways that damage their life prospects, they reveal an absence of conscious control over their existence. But this absence of control is not merely debilitating. It is also the basis for the subject's ability to become other than it is. The primacy of the alien within — the unconscious — makes freedom possible. Freedom depends on the unconscious getting in the way of our ability to realize our conscious wants.

We typically think of the unconscious as the site of unfreedom. When we act unconsciously, we don't deliberate on a course of action and experience the act of choosing it. But freedom is not the result of conscious deliberation. It is the ability to interrupt the path of determination that would otherwise govern our existence. This is precisely what the unconscious does. In the face of social or psychic determinants, the unconscious inaugurates a break and forges an alternate possibility that has no social or psychic precursor. It is because it evades our conscious control that the unconscious marks the point of the subject's freedom. We are free through our self-division.

It is not just subjectivity that lacks self-identity. No entity at all is simply self-identical. If one were, it would be incapable of development over time or even movement in space. This goes even for inanimate objects, like mountains or streams, as well as for plants and animals, whose temporal and spatial changes are more evident. If an entity simply was what it was, it would never undergo any change at all. This is how we know that no such entity exists.[5] But the subject of signification turns the absence of self-identity into the structure that defines it. This is the process of alienation.

The name is the first mark of alienation that most people receive. No child initially names itself.[6] A name stands for an act of violence that some authority perpetrates on an incipient person. Parents or other adults impose an alien name on a child, either arbitrarily or in the spirit of what they believe will best approximate who the child is (and will become). Even if one experiences one's name as perfectly appropriate, as completely one's own, it remains an alien imposition. Others place a destiny on the child through the chosen name. Parents might name a child *Ernest* in hopes that it will grow to be honest and forthright. Or they might name a child *Grace* with the idea that it will become decorous and even elegant. Parents often employ the names of artists, such as *Langston* or *Dashiell*, so that their children can partake of genius by association. Most typically, however, we give children names that have a family history attached to them to remind the child of the lineage that should inform its future comportment. Even when the name has no significance at all, it remains an alien signifier attached to the child. In each case, the child does not choose its own name but confronts the name as an alien imposition. If the child comes to see the name as identical with itself, this only occurs after the initial alienation of the naming process.

Through the name, one relates to oneself from a clear distance. Every language has a way of identifying oneself by indicating one's name. In English, I say, "My name is Todd." Or in German, "*Ich heiße Todd.*" Or in Spanish, "*Me llamo Todd.*" No matter what the linguistic variation, in each case the statement proclaiming identity simultaneously indicates an internal distance between the speaking subject and the name.[7] The sentence proclaiming the identity necessarily also betrays the distance as it reveals the separation between *ich* and *Todd*. If I were a self-identical and nonalienated being, I would not be able to say so.

The alienating status of the name remains even when one renames oneself. Instead of imagining myself as *Todd*, I identify more with the name *Theo* and change my name. When I take this step, I name myself rather than relying on the name that others have given to me. This would seem to overcome the alienation inherent in the name. But the problem remains. Even though I name myself, I do so with possibilities that come from others. I select among the group of names that people have used in the past or combine different ones to form my own. The choice of a name always involves a debt to an external authority. My new name not only comes from others, but I choose it to make an impression on them. No matter where it comes from, the name names my self-division.

The advantage that alienation confers is that it gives us some purchase on our self-division. Rather than just suffering this self-division until it eventually spells our doom, we can relate to it, manipulate it, and even augment it. Through the act of taking up our alienation instead of constantly trying to overcome it, its status undergoes a transformation. From seeing our alienation as a burden to overcome, we begin to view it as what frees us from what we are. Revising the negative judgment regarding alienation is a crucial political task, especially in an era that proffers endless schemes for overcoming it.

Alienation's bad rap stems from the image of completeness that lurks behind it. We imagine this completeness existing in a lost past such as the Garden of Eden or in a utopian future still to be attained. No matter what the scenario, completeness appears outside our immediate grasp. This is why it seduces us. This state without any alienation at all calls to us amid our alienation as a much more appealing alternative. But it remains appealing only so long as we imagine it abstractly. Any attempt to give concrete outlines to existence without alienation quickly shows the bankruptcy of this line of thought.[8]

One of the challenges of being subjects of alienation is that we must try to conceive of alienation without any reference to completeness or self-identity. We are alienated, but not from anything that could possibly make us whole. Equally, we have not lost anything that deprived us of an original wholeness. Thinking about lack without reference to wholeness changes the political valence of lack and alienation. Despite how it sounds, alienation exists without reference to a state that isn't alienated.

Alienation is the source of all human suffering — if we weren't alienated, we wouldn't suffer — but it is also the source of all satisfaction. Without alienation, we would exist bereft of anything that makes life worth living because we would lack the space in which to act contrary to what was given. Subjects would be nothing but the forces that produced them. Alienation creates an opening for every enjoyable activity — from having sex to eating cake to discussing German Idealism.

What separates speaking beings from the rest of the universe is their ability to grasp their own lack of self-identity. Language gives subjects the ability to recognize their own alienation as what constitutes them as who they are. The distance that language introduces into the speaking being changes its relationship to alienation. Subjects of the signifier can recognize themselves as alienated and take up their own alienation. They can find satisfaction in their lack of self-identity rather than just perishing from it. But the refusal to see alienation as constitutive works against this possibility.

We most often think of our existential and political projects as attempts to overcome alienation. Although there are important exceptions, most of our struggles target alienation as something they hope to eradicate. Therapists imagine that they help patients to attain self-identity. Political revolutionaries strive for a society in which they can live in harmony with others. Ecological activists work toward a future form of existence that will be in touch with the rest of the natural world.[9] Despite the radical diversity of these projects, alienation is in each case what they work to stamp out, though it might not be named as such. In the predominant ways of thinking, alienation is the problem to be overcome, not what enables all struggle in the first place.

This book represents a completely different take on alienation. Its claim is that the effort to overcome alienation is not a radical response to the current state of things but a failure to see the constitutive power of alienation for us. Instead of trying to overcome alienation and accede to an unalienated existence, we should redeem alienation as an existential and political program. Alienation is emancipation.

Chapter One
The Disturbed Subject

Identity for Sale

A subject is not the symbolic identity that corresponds to it. To understand how alienation operates, it helps to start with this basic disjunction between subjectivity and identity. Identity consists of the various social positions that one occupies: job, familial status, religious affiliation, political preference, ethnicity, and so on. No matter how much I see myself as any or all of these identities, I am never fully identical with them. This failure is subjectivity. No matter how I might mold them to fit myself, none of these identities can fully coincide with my subjectivity.

Subjectivity comes into existence through a process of alienation that produces a divide between the subject and the symbolic identity that it takes on in the social order. As a subject, no one can become identical with a symbolic identity because the subject relates to this identity from a distance. There is always a divide between who I am as a subject and what I am as an identity. No matter how perfectly I manage to fit my symbolic identity, the very effort that I employ to do so will testify to the existence of a disjunction.[1] If subjectivity could be reduced to a symbolic identity, there would be no need to engage in identification.

Subjectivity is undefinable. Who we are as subjects is a problem that has no solution. Even though we constantly make efforts to respond to it, it is a question that has no answer. Symbolic identity of whatever stripe — man, woman, Chinese, Italian, Hindu, Muslim, lawyer, dentist — constructs an answer to this question, a solution to this problem. When I feel rudderless as an existing subject, I remind myself that I'm an American or that I'm a son or that I'm a professor in an attempt to regain my bearings and assure myself about what I am. But no matter how much effort I expend to identify with a symbolic position, I cannot traverse the distance between my subjectivity and this identity.[2] I'm left with a failure to fit in.[3]

Symbolic identity provides markers of what one is to plaster over the question of who one is. This obfuscation is not avoidable: there is no subjectivity without a symbolic identity attached to it. It is impossible to avoid having an identity. This is what allows us to have a way of relating to others and of navigating our social situation.

At the same time, symbolic identity, despite being unavoidable, is a flight from subjectivity. We seek respite from the problem of subjectivity in the promised security of our symbolic identity. The necessary failure of identity to provide this security doesn't lessen our proclivity to seek it out continually for what it promises. Our political being depends on the relationship that we adopt to our symbolic identity.

We have the ability to confront our symbolic identity from the perspective of our alienated subjectivity. Although it might seem modest or even ineffectual, this is a political act — and the basis for all more ambitious political activity. It is the first and most important political act that one can accomplish because it enables one to act beyond the strict confines of one's symbolic universe.

Sinking into a symbolic identity, in contrast, allows one to avoid confronting political questions as political. These questions appear to have ready-made answers from the perspective of a symbolic identity. In this sense, symbolic identity is always an avoidance of the problem of emancipation. This is a point that Alenka Zupančič stresses in *What IS Sex?* According to Zupančič, "(emancipatory) politics begins with 'loss of identity,' and there is nothing deplorable in this loss."[4] Identity enacts a depoliticization of the subject. All identity is conformist.

When it adopts — or attempts to adopt — an identity, the subject always conforms because the forces of social authority establish every symbolic identity, even those that feel the most transgressive to those occupying them. While the subject's unconscious desire is always askew in relation to the social authority's demands, through identification the subject tries to model itself on some form of authority and find assurance in the authority's approval. Unconscious desire occurs without the authority's support, but every symbolic identity also seeks social recognition. One takes on a symbolic identity in order to have that identity recognized by some social authority, which restricts the ability of symbolic identity to mount a political challenge to the forces of social authority. It doesn't help if there is a dissonance among one's different symbolic identities because every such identity has its basis in social recognition. No matter how radical it imagines itself, it ultimately seeks someone's approval.

The political distinction between subjectivity and symbolic identity becomes apparent whenever a dicey social issue arises. For instance, if a person asks me my views on the death penalty, rather than think through all the permutations of the issue and come to some conclusion, I can rely on whatever symbolic identity I see as my own. I can consider the teachings of the Catholic Church and tell my interlocutor that I'm opposed to the death penalty on that basis. Or I can point out that my parents raised me according to the strict code of the Ten Commandments that lead me to see the death penalty as an expression of justice. I might even have recourse to my identity as a political liberal to find a ground for opposing this harsh punishment. In each of these cases, some form of symbolic identity provides an exit from the burden of subjectivity. Identity supplies ways to resolve the existential problem that subjectivity poses. Whenever I don't know what to think or how to act, my identification with a specific symbolic position intervenes to guide me toward a clear answer.

The move from subjectivity to identity covers the gaps left by questions with no readymade answers. Identity gives the subject an orientation in the world, a way of understanding how to respond to existential questions (such as what constitutes the proper punishment for heinous acts). It's for this reason that people seek out the refuge of symbolic identity. But as a subject, I must face the question of capital punishment without the security and guidance that symbolic identity provides. This doesn't mean that I cannot have a specific view on this issue, just that identity cannot provide support for this view.

Symbolic identity is so appealing precisely because it offers a path to escape one's subjectivity.[5] The search for an identity that fully corresponds to who we are is an attempt to cure alienation. Identity obscures the alienation of subjectivity by making the subject appear reducible to its identity. While the subject is out of joint with itself, identity creates the appearance of self-coincidence, even if an identity is one of permanent flux. By recognizing every identity as a failure, we can remain within the question of subjectivity itself. This is possible due to the misalignment between the subject and the identity attached to it. The subject comes to the fore as it finds itself outside its own being and distinct from its own identity, no matter how much this identity seems to belong to it.

Speech inserts a distance within the being that speaks. Subjectivity is this internal distance, this inability to be fully oneself. The subject relates to itself through the mediation of the signifier and, as a result, must relate to what it is from the outside rather than simply being what it is. Although the signifier forms the basis for symbolic identity, it also highlights a crack within the natural being that forces the subject to take up a position relative to what it is. Every signifier is dialectical. Through subjection to the signifier, a being gains the ability to think its own negation. As Joan Copjec states in *Read My Desire*, "Signification gives rise inevitably to doubt, to the possibility of its own negation; it enables us to think the annihilation, the full-scale destruction of our entire signified reality."[6] There is no subjectivity without the possibility of negation, the possibility of rejecting not only the signification that one has in the social order but also the entire symbolic universe. For the alienated subject, everything given can be questioned and dismissed. Even when one affirms one's signification, this can only occur through the failure of any self-identity.

For instance, when the subject identifies itself as a German, it simultaneously attests to its nonidentity with Germanness. The most unequivocal identification with one's Germanness cannot help but affirm Germanness as an identity distinct from the subject that must take it up. If Germanness were not distinct from the subject who takes it up, no act of identification would be necessary or even possible. The act of asserting the absence of difference testifies to the difference. Self-identification with signifiers is simultaneously self-distancing, although we aren't typically aware of this. One uses terms that are not one's own — no one invents the signifiers of self-description — to define oneself. The act of asserting what one is always attests to one's distance from what one is. That is, it attests to one's alienation.

Marine Le Pen, leader of the Rassemblement National party in France, is invested in being French and in what it means to be French. For her, France is a Catholic nation that should be economically independent from other nations. The traditions of France, including its language, separate it from the rest of Europe and from Muslim nations. But no matter how invested Le Pen is in French identity, she cannot avoid the distinction between herself and the French identity that she embraces. Her articulation of this identity establishes it as distinct from herself and not completely identical. No one is more ensconced in the tradition of France than Le Pen, and yet, even she must strive to root herself in her Frenchness.

The mere act of articulating a description of oneself evinces an internal gap. If the subject were identical with Frenchness, it would not require any proclamation or signifier of identity. The signifier of identity indicates that the subject is not what it claims to be because it reveals that the subject has to perform this identity rather than just being it. The subject's identity is always outside itself. The subject has to take up this identity through repeated acts of identification, none of which firmly cement the identity so that it never needs to be articulated again. No one just belongs to the symbolic structure that houses them.

Many science-fiction films focus on this breach between the subject and its identity. In *Blade Runner* (Ridley Scott, 1981), *Total Recall* (Paul Verhoeven, 1990), and *Dark City* (Alex Proyas, 1998), we see the distance made manifest narratively.[7] In each of these films, characters discover that what is most intimate to them — their memories — has been imposed on them by an external (malevolent) force. The films expose symbolic identity as foreign to subjectivity. For instance, Doug Quaid (Arnold Schwarzenegger) in *Total Recall* becomes aware that the person he used to be, Carl Hauser (also Arnold Schwarzenegger), constructed the identity of Quaid to penetrate and ultimately destroy the rebellion on the planet Mars. Everything that Quaid knows of his own identity is false, the result of Hauser's manipulative construction. His identity is nothing but this external manipulation. While at the end of the film Quaid breaks from Hauser's control and frees himself, he is left with no identity of his own at all distinct from the identity that Hauser implanted in him. There is no symbolic identity for him to fall back on that would provide a basis for his future life. Quaid resonates so much as a character because he makes explicit the situation of every subject.

Although there is no external force implanting fake memories in us, we are all nonetheless the kin of Doug Quaid (albeit without Arnold Schwarzenegger's physique).[8] That is, we are subjects relating to an identity that we can never become completely identical with because it is absolutely foreign to our subjectivity. Quaid must struggle with who he is as a subject apart from his symbolic identity. Unlike the spectators of the film, he cannot simply relate to this identity from a distance but must reject it altogether as a fabrication. In this sense, Quaid illustrates what alienated subjectivity would be without any symbolic identity whatsoever to fall back on. Quaid is the paradigm of subjectivity, someone who lives out an unadulterated alienation without any possibility of investing himself in his symbolic identity. If we cannot be Doug Quaid, all the worse for us.[9]

The external status of identity — the subject's lack of immediate self-identity — produces an unconscious that speaks outside of the subject's conscious control. The unconscious emerges out of the gap between the subject and its identity — between who the subject is and what it is. The split between subjectivity and symbolic identity aligns with the split between the unconscious and consciousness. Although not all symbolic identity is conscious, it represents an attempt to escape the problem of the unconscious, which is what is alien within subjectivity.

Appetite for Destruction

A divide exists between what we mean and what we say, between our intention and our act, or between consciousness and the unconscious. We are alienated beings because what we say articulates our desire rather than what we mean. In the same way, our acts display who we are despite what we intend. The unconscious is not our own private secret but what we constantly demonstrate to others through our speech and acts. Others always know our unconscious better than we do ourselves: they see it in action where we cannot. We confront the truth of our subjectivity in speech and actions, but it appears to us only in an alien form, as what we do not will or intend.

Unconscious desire is not simply a desire that escapes the awareness of consciousness. It is a desire that consciousness cannot take up as its own because it violates the logic of consciousness. The unconscious is another scene that follows a logic distinct from that of consciousness. A fundamental divide exists between the subject's conscious wishes and its unconscious desires. No amount of reflection on the subject's part can overcome this split. Even those who are fully aware of its existence end up succumbing to the unconscious desire that undermines their conscious wish. This split leaves the subject constantly at odds with itself. Freud discovers the effect of the split in psychoanalysis when he stumbles on the negative therapeutic reaction.

When recounting therapeutic failures, Freud has recourse to the power of the unconscious in relation to the conscious will. A patient wills to get better, but the unconscious finds its own satisfaction in the disorder and thus fights to sustain it. According to Freud, "The satisfaction of this unconscious sense of guilt is perhaps the most powerful bastion in the subject's (usually composite) gain from illness — in the sum of forces which struggle against his recovery and refuse to surrender his state of illness."[10] When it comes to the unconscious, the failures of psychoanalytic treatment teach Freud much more than its successes. Patients come close to overcoming their disorder, but this leads them to double down on it, despite their conscious will to get better. The negative therapeutic reaction, which is what Freud calls this development, testifies to the primacy of the unconscious in the division of the subject. The primacy of the unconscious in subjectivity is the mark of alienation.

Consciously, subjects wish to pursue their own self-interest and further their own good. They establish aims that promise to produce happiness. I try to live in a comfortable apartment, work at an interesting job, watch engaging television programs, and eat decadent desserts, all in the belief that these will bring me happiness. At no point do I consciously set out to be unhappy, even if I'm doing something that others might find disgusting, like eating raw oysters or mud wrestling.

The great theorist of the structure of conscious wishes is Blaise Pascal. He grasps the central role that the wish for happiness plays in the subject's conscious life. As Pascal famously notes, "All men seek to be happy. This is without exception, whatever different means they use. They all strive toward this end…. This is the motive of every action of every man, even of those who go hang themselves."[11] Pascal concludes this analysis of the ubiquitous human pursuit of happiness with those who commit suicide to underline its complete ubiquity. For Pascal, there is no way to avoid seeking happiness — or pursuing one's own self-interest. That pursuit, as he sees it, inheres in our very being.

If we confine ourselves to consciousness, Pascal's analysis is convincing. As a conscious being, the subject seeks happiness through the pursuit of its self-interest. Everything that this conscious being does is self-interested. There is no path for consciousness to avoid this pursuit, even when it opts for self-destruction. The structure of consciousness is organized around the subject's will, not its desire. But unconscious desire is the blind spot in Pascal's theorization of the will to happiness, the reason why Pascal is no longer a convincing thinker in the contemporary universe. Although the subject consciously wishes to be happy, it cannot avoid unconsciously desiring to sustain itself as alienated, which requires continued acts of self-destruction. Pascal's theory of a universal will to happiness stumbles over the alienated status of the subject. If we were what we were, Pascal would be right. But the disjunction within subjectivity leads to acts that don't promote human happiness. Not only is the subject alienated from itself, it desires to sustain its alienation at any cost.[12]

The uniqueness of the subject doesn't lie in consciousness. One could imagine — and science-fiction films have imagined — an exact duplication of someone's consciousness. But what always escapes duplication is how the subject relates to its conscious wishes. This way of relating to consciousness is the unconscious, which is the basis of the subject's singularity. The unconscious distances us from consciousness, and it is through this distance that we are distinct as subjects. Subjects stick out from the natural world and from their culture because their unconscious never permits them simply to be what they are. The unconscious is how who we are subjectively exceeds what we are symbolically.[13] The alienation that corresponds to our unconscious is irreducible to everything that influences us, unlike our conscious wishes.

Subjects consciously will to be happy, but they unconsciously find satisfaction in undermining their conscious will. Satisfaction depends on preventing the achieving of happiness because finally achieving the happiness that the subject consciously seeks exposes that this happiness does not exist. Happiness cannot be a present state. Attaining one's object reveals that this object is never the equivalent of what one desired. As a result, happiness can never be anything but the promise of future happiness. Unconscious desire works in conjunction with the conscious wish for happiness by undermining the possibility of its achievement, thereby preserving the dream of a happiness to come.

The unconscious finds satisfaction in creating and sustaining alienation because there is no initial satisfying object. The subject discovers a satisfying object only through a loss that gives the subject something to desire. Rather than imagining desire as a natural phenomenon, we should see it as a structure that has to emerge out of the relationship between bodily needs and social demands. By undermining the conscious pursuit of happiness, unconscious desire keeps itself going by continually erecting an obstacle to the fulfillment of the wish. Unconscious desire satisfies itself by opposing the conscious wish.

The unconscious accompanies each of the subject's statements and adds a layer of significance to them that the subject does not intend. For the speaking subject imbued with an unconscious, there is no innocent statement of fact. The subject's unconscious desire informs every statement that the subject makes. Even the most apparently innocent comment bears the stain of an unconscious desire that drives the subject to make the comment. When I say to my neighbor that the ominous clouds portend rain, I do not just make a weather prediction (although I also do that). The reason why I announce this prediction to my neighbor always lurks in the background of the bare statement and undermines its innocence. Perhaps I am telling my neighbor about the upcoming rain to spoil her anticipation of a picnic planned for that day because I envy her pleasure. Or maybe the remark serves to forge a bond between fellow sufferers who must endure the horrible weather of our region together. Most likely, however, I use the banal weather comment as a way of navigating the trauma of the encounter with the neighbor. I say something meaningless rather than reveal that I have nothing to say in the confrontation with the alienating force of the neighbor's subjectivity. It doesn't matter which of these scenarios is accurate. In either event, some unconscious desire informs even the most innocuous remark about the weather and, what's more, every statement that the subject makes. The distortion of desire is inescapable for the speaking subject.

This distortion manifests itself in my interpretation of the statements of others as well. If a friend tells me that my apartment looks nice, I do not simply accept this as a statement of fact. Instead, I wonder why my friend said this and respond to the remark in this light. Perhaps she was preparing me for a request to borrow money; perhaps she thought my apartment usually looks dirty and noticed the change; perhaps she prefers untidy friends and will use this as a pretext for breaking off her relationship with me. There are many possibilities and typically no clear desire hidden within the statement, but it is impossible for me simply to take the statement at face value. Even a straightforward declaration of the cleanliness of my apartment that has no conscious manipulative intent to it has the baggage of an unconscious desire. Subjects must desire to speak, or else they would avoid speaking — and even silence doesn't escape desire because it takes place against the background of speaking. If my friend stays silent rather than complimenting my apartment, I will still ponder the meaning of this silence, just as I pondered the meaning of the compliment.[14] Because the subject is an alienated being, it cannot speak without distorting what it says with the stain of its unconscious desire. Even though those who first theorize the subject do so without any consideration of the unconscious, they still root subjectivity in its necessary alienation.

Why Kant I Be Me?

The origin of the philosophical use of the term *subject* reveals its intrinsic connection with alienation. When thinkers talk

WHY WE SHOULDN'T TRY TO FIND OURSELVES

about the subject, they necessarily talk about the alienated subject even if they don't mention or stress alienation. No one starts to talk about the subject philosophically until self-division becomes included in its conception. This subject always has an internal distance from itself, which is why theorists use this term rather than the more readily comprehensible options, such as self, individual, person, or human being. These terms are all more straightforward and involve less theoretical jargon, which is a good reason to prefer them. But they lack what is most important about the subject. While one can always specify that one is talking about a divided self or a divided individual, *subject*, in contrast to these other terms, implies self-division — and thus alienation. Implicit in the term is the fact that there is no such thing as an unalienated subject, no subject that is not a subject of alienation. This is apparent in the case of the first major figure to use the term in the sense that we understand it today.

Immanuel Kant did not invent the term *subject* (or *Subjekt*, in German), but he might as well have.[15] In the *Critique of Pure Reason* and subsequent writings, he popularizes its use as a philosophical concept in a new sense. It's fair to say that Kant is the first philosopher of the subject, although, for some reason, this does not receive any theoretical attention. Beginning with Kant, *subject* no longer refers simply to a grammatical entity (the subject of the sentence) or one in a subordinate position relative to another (one subject to a monarch).[16] These are the senses in which prior thinkers, such as Baruch Spinoza and Gottfried Leibniz, employ the term. But after the Kantian revolution, the term *subject* comes to refer to the entity that relates negatively to itself, one that is never just what it is.[17]

Kant has recourse to subjectivity when he wants to separate the entity that he calls the subject from the rest of the world.

For this reason, subjectivity is always alienated subjectivity for Kant, even if he never makes this explicit by using the term *alienation* or any equivalent.[18] As Kant sees it, the subject can never find itself at home in the world because it constitutes its world through the act of transcendental imagination. Without this act whereby the subject gives itself a world with which to relate, there would be no world at all but rather a mass of indifferent data input. Instead of existing within its world, the subject constitutes the world of its experience. Subjectivity is the condition of the possibility of experience. Kant doesn't reject the existence of the external world — he carefully distinguishes himself from George Berkeley, especially in the second edition of the *Critique of Pure Reason* — but he does contend that this world receives its coherence through the subject's transcendental act.[19]

When Kant describes toward the beginning of the *Critique of Pure Reason* how the faculty of sensibility works to structure our intuitions, the term *subject* makes a dramatic appearance. Sensibility is one of three faculties — the others are the understanding and reason — through which the subject gives coherence to the world that it experiences. Kant's use of the term *subject* enables him to express that the entity he describes must act on itself in order to have an experience that makes sense to it. In Kant's idiom, to refer to the subject is to indicate a being separated from itself and thus capable of acting on itself. The subject gives itself the forms of space and time for the intuitions that arrive through sensibility.

As the source of space and time, the subject (as Kant conceives it) cannot belong spatially or temporally to the world. The world is not, for Kant, inherently spatial or temporal, since these forms are the contributions that subjectivity brings to its encounter with externality. After making this point about space, Kant comes to the same conclusion about time. During this discussion, he refers to the subject as the basis of the experience of temporality. According to Kant, "Time is... merely a subjective condition of our (human) intuition (which is always sensible, i.e., insofar as we are affected by objects), and in itself, outside the subject, is nothing. Nonetheless it is necessarily objective in regard to all appearances, thus also in regard to all things that can come before us in experience."[20] Although the form of temporality derives from the subject, it is not subjective in the sense that one could opt for it or not. It gives our experience a requisite form that structures it for us, which is why Kant insists on time as objective rather than merely subjective. But the forms of space and time also show that the subject is necessarily out of place and out of time in its existence. Subjectivity can be responsible for temporality because the subject is not itself subjected to time.

The Kantian subject is its self-division. It is self-conscious because it relates to itself from a distance rather than just being identical with what it is. Its self-division manifests itself most significantly in subjectivity's relationship to freedom and determination. Rather than theorizing the subject as either free or determined, Kant insists — and believes that he proves — that the subject is free and determined at the same time. The point is not that some of the subject's actions are free while external causes determine others but that every action is simultaneously free and determined. When one considers the subject from a theoretical point of view, it is determined. But when one thinks of it from a practical standpoint, as a being in action, it is free. The attempt to discern which of these approaches accurately apprehends the truth of the subject misses Kant's point, which is that both are equally true.[21]

The subject can be free and determined at the same time

only as a result of the subject's fundamental alienation. Kant's subject is so divided from itself that one can think this subject from the perspective of theory or from the perspective of practice. But one cannot think the two together: theory and practice are strictly incompatible in Kant's philosophy. While later German Idealists would attempt to unify these two distinct poles in the Kantian system, doing so, from Kant's perspective, risks domesticating the radical alienation of the subject from itself. When a thinker such as J. G. Fichte attempts to locate the theoretical perspective within the practical one, his subject appears more unified than Kant's, despite the fact that Fichte theorizes away certain persistent problems in Kant's philosophy.

The division in Kant's thought between his theoretical work (articulated in the *Critique of Pure Reason*) and his practical work (most famously laid out in the *Critique of Practical Reason*) stands in for the alienation of the subject in his philosophy. These two strains of his philosophy do not simply exist side by side. They have an alien and even contradictory relation to each other. For the theoretical Kant, the practical Kant represents an overstepping of what it should be possible to think. But for the practical Kant, the theoretical marks a retreat from the problem of the subject's freedom. One cannot simply choose one side over the other but must think both together, despite their incompatibility. Alienation is so central to the Kantian subject that it infects even the corpus of Kant's philosophy. As Kant sees it, the alienation of the subject is not a problem to overcome. It is the definition of subjectivity.

Broken Animals

Failing to take alienation into account leads to an inevitable misunderstanding of how politics works. We are political beings not due to a party affiliation but as a result of a slanted relation to the social order. To be political is not to be neutral. Every subject is a political being because of the distortion it suffers at the hands of signification, because of its fundamental alienation. Alienation constitutes our political being. We don't escape our political being by opting out of it or by entering a situation that appears depoliticized. We cannot be stripped of our alienation, which means that we cannot lose our political being or somehow escape it. No subject can be reduced to the biological entity that constitutes its material basis.[22] The point is not that the subject bears no relationship to the human animal but that the signifying distortion that produces the subject so fundamentally changes the animal that we must take alienation as a starting point for making sense of what we do. Despite our status as biological entities, we have a capacity for acting unnaturally that derives from our alienation. Our unnatural proclivities trump the physiological imperatives acting on us.

Thinking of subjects as natural or as cultural entities — or as a mixture of the two — elides their alienated status. To view subjectivity as the product of natural or cultural forces is to strip it of its inherently political being, which is equivalent to subjectivity's irreducibility to what determines it. In the wake of the transformation that occurs through naturalizing or culturalizing subjectivity, subjects continue to be political (because they can't help but be), but their political bearing becomes invisible (because we have theorized it away). Political decisions are naturalized or culturalized, seen as expressions of innate self-interest rather than as acts of a free subject. The alienated subject is not a self-interested being that always responds according to what best advances its prospects. What define subjectivity are its unconscious efforts to sabotage its self-interest, its proclivity for finding ways of giving itself difficulties.

Subjectivity is not a privilege that we must combat, a privilege that renders one a master and possessor of the rest of the natural world.[23] It is instead what alienates a being from the natural world, what makes it impossible for it to master or possess this world. Because subjectivity is always alienated, far from mastering the world, it is necessarily in a skewed relation to the world. To be a subject is always to relate to one's world from a distance.[24]

The subject has its basis in a natural being, but subjectivity is a distortion of this being. The result is a being that has become something unnatural or denaturalized. This denaturalization is the basis of the subject's political being. But the image of subjectivity rooted in nature has misled thinkers for centuries. When he attempts to define the political being of humanity, Aristotle has recourse to the natural world and the human relationship to it. Early on in the *Politics*, he provides the most well-known definition of the role of politics in human existence. Aristotle writes, "Man is by nature a political animal."[25] The problem with Aristotle's formulation is that the political being of subjects, as he understands it, is the direct result of their position within the natural world rather than their alienation from it. Even though Aristotle sees our political being as exceptional in relation to other animals (and thus as a source of human privilege), he fails to see the fundamental role that alienation plays in constituting the political being of the subject. In this way, Aristotle naturalizes the speaking subject's political being. This interpretation has the ideological effect of dulling the contradictions that emerge within the social order and within subjectivity itself, contradictions that Plato's human exceptionalism preserves.[26]

Aristotle's vision of politics is not one of antagonistic struggle but of coming together for the sake of general well-being. He identifies no antagonism between master and slave or between man and woman. This permits the oppression of the latter figures to function unimpeded in his political philosophy. There is a direct throughline from Aristotle's belief in the natural status of humanity to his philosophical decision to keep slaves and women in their secondary place.[27]

The insistence on continuity with the natural world rather than the subject's thoroughgoing break from it gives Aristotle cover to naturalize and justify relations of inequality within politics. Just as there is inequality in the natural world, there is inequality in the human world. Rather than uprooting itself from any natural being, juridical law, for Aristotle, functions like natural law. It defines relations that already exist. It does not command that subjects act against themselves.

Aristotle's acceptance of the inevitability of inequality follows from his investment in continuity and lack of awareness of the subject's alienation from the natural world. Any attempt to root subjectivity in its natural being will end up justifying social inequality, even if this is not the explicit intent. When we conceive ourselves as natural beings, the argument for equality founders on the fact of natural inequality: Florence runs faster than Inge, while Bob is smarter than Carl and Kareem is taller than Calvin. A clear inequality dominates our natural relations with each other, but fortunately, we never remain in natural relations with each other, which is what Aristotle fails to account for.

Conceiving of equality requires embracing a denaturalized, alienated subject. It is only by conceiving the subject not as naturally political but as political through its violent break from the natural world that we can insist on the equality of all subjects. The danger is that we will see political contestation as a field of pure differences competing with each other to advance their own interests. It is only by insisting on the subject's unnatural status that we can conceive of it as a political being capable of antagonistic struggle on behalf of freedom and equality. How we conceive of subjectivity determines how we constitute the political field and the political possibilities that will be available to us, which is why this question is not just a theoretical one.

Even if we insist on the break between the subject and its natural being, there remains an obvious link between the two. The subject has an animal body and necessarily comes from natural origins. When one becomes a subject, one does not cease to be an animal or to suffer the ultimate demise that affects all animals. One remains prone to disease and bodily damage. In the passage from animal to subject, animality continues to accompany the subject throughout its existence. But animality is not a mode of being alongside subjectivity. For the subject, there is never any pure form of animality. The distorting power of subjectivity reaches into all aspects of the subject's animal being.

Alienation distances the subject from its animal being, but this distancing constitutes the subject as a different type of entity, one that otherwise would not exist. Subjectivity is not the result of an evolutionary process but of a rupture introduced by the signifier into the realm of animality. Even though we can assume that signification emerged for evolutionary reasons, its effects violate the imperatives of natural selection and even survival. The signifying rupture is not simply the triumph of culture over nature. Subjectivity lingers between nature and culture.[28]

Perverse Satisfactions

The alienation of subjectivity reproduces itself in excessive acts that it performs to compensate for its lack of self-identity. Or one could say that the failure of identity leads to overidentification. The subject becomes a figure of excess in response to its alienation, and this opens new paths to satisfaction. Because the subject cannot find a truly satisfying food, it eats too much. Because the subject cannot have purely reproductive sex, it invents a plethora of perverse sexual acts. For subjects, both eating and sex become detached from their animal function. Though they continue to fill biological needs, a complete reversal renders biology secondary, so that biology no longer plays a role in the satisfaction that eating and sex provide.

In each case, in fact, biological need can interfere with the satisfaction of the subject's alienated desire. Almost everyone has had this experience with eating. The foods that I know will best satisfy my biological needs — basically green leafy vegetables and legumes — do not arouse my desire to eat. Chocolate doughnuts, on the other hand, compel my desire to such an extent that I must make an effort to stop myself from eating them, even though they have a deleterious effect on my biological functioning. Even if there are evolutionary reasons informing this choice, the satisfaction that it brings, separate from the pleasure of the taste, bespeaks desire's detachment from biology. The deleterious effect on the body that a food has renders it more satisfying to eat. We desire that which doesn't address our biological needs.[29]

When one considers sexuality, the divorce between desire and biology becomes even clearer. As women have begun to have children later in life, the idea of scheduling sex for the moment of ovulation has become popular. Couples calculate when the woman is ovulating, and they have sex at this time to maximize the odds of producing a child. If the satisfaction that derives from sex were the satisfaction of reproducing oneself and fulfilling a biological need to reproduce, one would imagine that these targeted sex events would be the most satisfying imaginable. But even if one has not participated in such an activity, it does not require a great feat of imagination to understand that this is not the case. Having sex just to produce a baby has the effect of eliminating the pleasure of the activity. It becomes the performance of an onerous duty that deprives one of the satisfaction that usually accompanies sex. Having purely reproductive sex is akin to eating a diet consisting solely of raw kale.

If we define perversion as the decoupling of an instinct from its purely biological function, then all subjects are perverse in their eating and their sexuality.[30] The satisfaction that both eating and sex produce for the speaking subject stems from the distance between these acts and the biological needs that they fulfill. Those who enjoy overeating binge not on the foods that will most effectively contribute to their survival but on those that will potentially kill them. They eat, for example, cookies, cake, and ice cream. Those who devote themselves to sex do not invent acts that will best ensure reproduction but ones that evince the distance between sex and reproduction. They try masturbation, fellatio, cunnilingus, anal sex, group sex, and multiple variations of these. Just as no overeater has ever binged on broccoli, no sex addict has ever overdosed on reproductive sex.

Attempts to explain overeating or sex addiction with recourse to biological causes are commonplace. For instance, rather than theorizing obesity as the result of the subject's alienation, certain naturalistic thinkers see it as a development of an evolutionary mismatch. We developed proclivities for a situation that no longer exists, and the evolved characteristics that once worked to our advantage now threaten our survival. According to evolutionary biologist Daniel Lieberman, "Millions of years of evolution favored ancestors who craved energy-rich foods, including simple carbohydrates like sugar which used to be rare, and who efficiently stored excess calories as fat."[31] Evolution prepared the human animal properly, but cultural changes worked faster than natural selection, resulting in widespread obesity in contemporary society. Scholars in all fields and most of the public tend to accept these interpretations as definitive. They accept that we are natural beings rather than alienated subjects.

Explanations of the subject's sexual excesses tend to follow those of its culinary excesses. Males cheat on their spouses because their genes want to spread themselves as widely as possible, whereas females opt for monogamy because their genes see this as the best strategy for helping their offspring to survive. In *How the Mind Works*, Steven Pinker offers a standard explanation for male promiscuity in terms of adaptation. He writes, "The more women a man has sex with, the more offspring he leaves; too much is never enough. That gives men a limitless appetite for casual sex partners (and perhaps for the commodities that in ancestral environments would have led to multiple partners, such as power and wealth)."[32] Natural selection can explain even the most extreme sexual acts because participation in them testifies to the fitness of the participant. There is no perversion so perverse that it cannot seem to be the result of the mechanism of adaptation rather than a product of the subject's alienation.

As if in an effort to validate this dictum, certain naturalistic thinkers have spent more energy than one might expect trying to discover the adaptive reasons for rape. Although many colleagues attacked them for their research, Randy Thornhill and Craig Palmer studied the causes for the evolution of rape. The result of their research, *A Natural History of Rape: Biological Bases of Sexual Coercion*, leaves open two different possibilities — one preferred by each of the co-authors. For Thornhill, rape is a result of adaptation, whereas for Palmer, it is a byproduct of the adaptive process. Though Thornhill and Palmer take pains to point out that the goal of their research is to arrive at better mechanisms for the prevention of rape, the very concept of rape as a biological inheritance landed them immediately in political hot water.[33]

Nonetheless, we should applaud Thornhill and Palmer for taking the mechanism of the naturalistic explanation to its end point in order to expose inadvertently its limitations. If it is the case that all of the subject's excesses are simply developments of its natural proclivities and not its alienation, this logic must apply to rape as well. Even if the pursuit of the naturalistic solution to rape seems politically inadvisable, the emergence of this line of thought follows directly from the fundamental assumption that humans are to be considered as animals rather than as subjects. All the actions of unalienated human animals, even the most excessive, must be natural and thus fit within the adaptive framework. Given the prominence of adaptive explanations, if Thornhill and Palmer did not theorize rape as an evolutionary adaptation, someone else would have done so. The problem with their approach is that it fails to consider the excessive violence of rape as the product of a perverse subjectivity, as the result of a subject finding enjoyment through the debasement of the other. From the perspective that drives Thornhill and Palmer, no perversion is so extreme that it departs from our natural being, and this gives rise to the demand for a natural explanation. But the question of rape, despite the thorniness of the political issue, is not the most difficult problem for naturalistic theorists to explain.

From the perspective of naturalistic thinking, the greatest perversion in human sexuality is not a masochist mutilating his own penis or a sadist torturing her victim prior to having sex with him. It is instead the fact that we remain alive after the age when sex serves a reproduction function. As anthropologist Peter Gray points out in his survey of the evolution of human sexuality, "The evolutionary puzzle remains why humans live beyond reproductive capacities."[34] According to naturalistic theory itself, the very life of the human animal is excessive. It outlives its optimal lifespan for the reproduction of its genes. But its excess in this regard goes further. Not only do humans live beyond their reproductive capacities, they also continue to engage in reproductive acts long after their reproductive potential has disappeared, as the high incidence of sexually transmitted infections in retirement communities indicates. If the elderly devoted themselves solely to their social function as grandparents, they would assist in optimizing the success of their own genes and those of humanity, but this is not all that they do. They also explore their own alienated subjectivity through sexual excesses, often more than they did when they were capable of reproducing.

The prevalence of sexually transmitted infections in retirement communities bespeaks the limitation of the explanatory power of conceiving subjects as natural beings. Neither the sexually active individual nor the species benefit from the sexual activity that produces these diseases because the female participants in the activity have passed the point of being able to reproduce. Though one can manage an explanation — most of the men are still capable of reproducing and simply lack viable targets for their genetic material — it appears makeshift and inadequate to the phenomenon. As is the case with the argument concerning rape, the phenomenon clearly violates the spirit of naturalism because its excessiveness seems so evidently purposeless from the standpoint of selection. People are having sex in retirement communities because they are alienated subjects driven to excesses by unconscious desires that don't correspond with their needs.

It is certainly possible to conceive of all the perversions associated with subjectivity as developments or offshoots of selection occurring in the human animal. Even when the case seems most strained (as in the case of elderly sex), one can nonetheless put forth a plausible argument that wins adherents. But these arguments ultimately seem inadequate to the phenomena they attempt to account for because they operate under the assumption that subjects, qua human animals, act for the sake of a fundamental self-interest and not in response to their fundamental alienation as subjects.

The perversions of subjectivity that defy explanation in terms of self-reproduction are not just exceptional cases found in a few isolated subjects who haven't managed to get with the program thanks to some miscoding in their genes. Instead, these perversions appear in every subject. What's more, they provide the means through which subjects satisfy themselves. The excesses of subjectivity are not akin to unnecessary organs like the appendix but rather give the subject its reason for continuing to exist. Whether it is a sexual practice, a type of food, or a particular overvalued object, the excessive attachment to what doesn't serve its self-interest satisfies the subject in a way that genetic self-reproduction does not. The irony of subjectivity is that if subjects could only reproduce themselves without their perverse excesses, they would have no desire to do so. They continue to exist as a result of the satisfaction that they derive from perversely violating the imperative of self-reproduction. Their self-reproduction depends on their refusal to follow the genetic impulse to reproduce themselves.

If subjects could simply pursue their own interest or their own good (or the good of their genes), they would belong to the world in which they exist. They would not be alienated. But the subject fails to belong because it constantly deviates from what would serve its good or the good of its world. The subject's failure to belong derives from its inherent perversity. As a result, one must view the subject's perversity, despite the horrors it has produced, as the key to the subject's singularity. Alienated subjectivity has a proclivity for perversion that makes the subject who it is.

The problem with naturalistic explanations of the subject's perversity is not just that they do not grasp the phenomenon adequately. Instead, the danger is that they mislead us about the status of the subject's excessiveness. From the perspective of human animality, excesses never appear excessive enough. The excesses of the human animal are just natural disturbances or imbalances that remain within the natural world out of which they emerge. This position fails to grant the subject's excess its proper radicality and thereby sustains the conception of subject as belonging to its world. The naturalistic explanation of perversity misses the fact that this perversity is the result of a denaturalized subjectivity, a subjectivity that is alien to itself. The subject's alienation frees it from the constraints of belonging to its world.

Even though the subject's alienation is responsible for terrible destruction in the world, our response to this alienation must involve its embrace. Without the alienation that denaturalizes the human animal, the subject would lack the singularity that gives its existence a value. When we misconceive of the subject's perversity as a natural deviation and try to explain it in those terms, we endanger the perversity itself by imagining that we might normalize this excess. But the subject's alienation is both the problem and the solution. We must reevaluate the subject's alienation as the basis for its ethical being.[35] Alienation leads to horror when we try to overcome it, but modernity opens up the possibility of the subject enduring its distance from itself.

Chapter Two
Displaced Modernity

To the Infinite and Beyond

The emergence of signification entails alienation. This alienation is not a historical phenomenon linked to a certain epoch in human history, such as that of capitalist modernity. People were not walking around happily unalienated when all of a sudden capitalists came along and imposed an alienating system on them. Alienation is unavoidable for the speaking being, no matter at what point in history this being exists because it is tied to the structure of signification rather than the nature of the social order. But despite its universality, the effects of alienation did not become fully evident until the scientific revolutions of modernity. This is why it makes sense for people to identify alienation with the modern epoch, even though this analysis does miss the mark. In modernity, the subject's lack of a place in which it belongs comes to the fore in a way that it could not in prior times. Alienation becomes evident in the modern universe. Rather than viewing the obviousness of alienation in modernity as a development to lament, it is one feature we should unapologetically celebrate about this period.

The discoveries of the modern epoch — heliocentrism, gravity, and relativity, to name just the most conspicuous —

all have an uprooting effect on subjectivity. They make people aware that there is no assigned place for subjectivity within the universe that modernity uncovers.[1] If there is no center of the universe and only an impersonal force holds everything together, then the subject has no way to understand its position in the order of things. It is an uprooted being without a terrain where it belongs. This distinguishes the modern universe from the traditional world, in which subjects could believe that they belonged where they were (and could psychically locate where they were). The discoveries of modernity indicate that the processes that constitute the universe go on regardless of subjectivity. Everything doesn't revolve around the subject or confirm the subject's belonging. In this universe, the subject does not fit because nothing fits.

As a modern subject, one must confront one's uprootedness. One has nowhere to go to feel at home. This is at once a devastating jolt and an emancipatory revelation. Subjectivity has always been ontologically homeless, but it is only in modernity that we can recognize this homelessness. There has never been a place for the subject, but in modernity the subject's displacement becomes foregrounded thanks to the discoveries that have occurred.

Although subjectivity didn't undergo any ontological transformation with the onset of modernity, it underwent an existential one. The experience of subjectivity began to shift when heliocentrism replaced geocentrism, which is why this revolution caused so much consternation among the religious authority figures of the time. When Nicolaus Copernicus challenged geocentrism and asserted that the Earth revolves around the Sun in *De revolutionibus orbium coelestium* in 1543, he upset the traditional position of subjectivity within the world, even if he did not intend to undermine ecclesiastical authority.[2]

While Copernicus moved the Earth out of the center of creation, the displacement of humanity was not in itself the source of our alienation. It is just as easy to experience oneself at home on the periphery as in the center.[3] The decentering of humanity does not necessarily imply uprooting. One can still have a place where one belongs while orbiting around a stable center, a fact that lessens the psychic blow of the Copernican heliocentric hypothesis.[4] The alienating force of the scientific revolution would occur later, when other scientists would take the implications of the heliocentric system beyond the conclusions of Copernicus.

Giordano Bruno was the first to break from the belief in a finite world and to posit an open universe that had no clear endpoint to it. In *Cause, Principle, and Unity*, he puts forward the hypothesis of infinite space in contrast to finitude inherent in both the geocentrism of Aristotle and Ptolemy as well as in the heliocentrism of Copernicus. Bruno contends, "The universe is … infinite and limitless, and consequently immobile."[5] With this claim, it ceases to be possible to orient oneself in a place because the absence of a limit gets in the way of establishing clear locations within space. In an infinite universe — or a universe without identifiable limits, which is how we would put it today — the alienation of subjectivity from place becomes more difficult to deny. Bruno paved the way in this direction, even more so than Copernicus, and other thinkers soon drew out implications that further highlight the subject's uprootedness.[6]

The modern universe has no locatable places. Entities have a place only in relation to each other, not against some foundational background. This influenced Johannes Kepler's analysis of star patterns. As Alexandre Koyré makes clear in *From the Closed World to the Infinite Universe*, once scientists theorize the infinity of space, it ceases to be possible to have an allotted position within that infinity. Even the stars lose their place. Koyré states that, "whereas for a finite world it is reasonable to choose a particular pattern [for the stars], the principle of sufficient reason prevents the geometrically minded God of Kepler from doing it in an infinite one."[7] The infinite universe cannot house definitive places because there is no possible reference point in infinity from which to nail down a location. Just as the stars can have no assigned place in an infinite universe, neither can Earth or those occupying it.

While it seems comforting to have a place of one's own or a home where one belongs, place is the index of one's lack of freedom. When everyone has a place, there is no possible conception of freedom.[8] Freedom is first of all the ability to leave one's assigned social place and move elsewhere.[9] Those who benefit from a social hierarchy try to assure that all remain in their assigned places, that place rules over existential uprootedness.[10] By disrupting the distribution of places, modernity creates an opening for freedom.

The lack of stable places in modernity is the basis for unprecedented social upheaval. The great emancipatory movements of modernity — from the slave revolt in Haiti to the rise of suffragist movements around the world — take displacement as their starting point. Even if the subjects driving these challenges to established regimes don't look up to the stars to confirm their lack of a place, they nonetheless refuse to remain in the social position assigned to them. As subjects of modernity, they revolt against the dominance of place.

Frantz Fanon is the great theorist of the rejection of place, the thinker who grasps most clearly how place is always oppressive. He recognizes the fundamental equality that modern displacement unleashes and calls on everyone to be adequate to the radicality of this displacement. In his attack on racist society, *Black Skin, White Masks*, he calls for a political break from the past. He writes, "I have not the right to put down roots. I have not the right to admit the slightest patch of being into my existence. I have not the right to become mired by the determinations of the past."[11] Fanon's conception of politics requires abjuring any of the comforts of a social or historical place. This is the basis for revolutionary action.

Embracing modernity's displacement does not require emigrating from one's native land or even moving out of one's hometown. Displacement is not nomadic. Kant was a displaced modern subject, and he never travelled very far from his hometown of Königsberg. Instead of physical travel, embracing modern displacement involves rejecting the conception of place conferring belonging on those who live there. The acceptance and embrace of one's failure to belong to any place is the basis of emancipation. Emancipation requires recognizing the appeal of displacement rather than longing for a home that no one has ever had.[12]

Breaking Up with Oneself

Emancipation is only on the table in the universe of modern science. The displacement that modern science uncovers makes possible the discovery of a displacement within people themselves. This internal displacement is alienated subjectivity. While internal displacement predates modern science, it becomes widely evident in modernity. This is a felicitous occurrence, not something to bemoan. Alienation separates the speaking subject from itself and allows it to act against the external factors that would otherwise determine its existence. But alienation can only be genuinely emancipatory when we recognize it.

Historically, societies offered speaking subjects an image of themselves that fit the traditions those societies maintained.[13] The belonging that characterized the premodern world might have given members of that world relative peace of mind about their status in it, but in doing so it deprived them of the singularity that stems from the emergence of the speaking subject. The subject's singularity is inextricable from its status as alienated both from its social milieu and from itself. Paradoxically, it is only through being distanced from itself that the subject can most be itself. One arrives at singularity only by giving up the lure of belonging.

The destruction of the illusion of belonging is the great accomplishment of modernity, even though it has often been woefully inadequate to this accomplishment. It frees the subject to experience the alienation that defines it as a speaking being by making evident the distance that separates the subject from that identity that purports to define the subject. As modern science displaces the subject, modern art reveals the ramifications of this displacement in its most radical form. Modern tragedy shows the alienated subject as a figure capable of defying its social position and all social positioning.

Shakespeare wrote his three most important tragedies at the beginning of the modern epoch. It is not coincidental that the first of these, *Hamlet*, was performed in 1600, the date that symbolically marks the dawn of modernity. Along with *Hamlet*, the tragedies *Othello* and *King Lear* also take the alienation of the subject in modernity as their primary focus. The characters in these plays are capable of tragic grandeur thanks to their inability to fit in their world or to achieve harmony with themselves. Even when the characters are diabolically evil, this evil stems from a fundamental disjunction within themselves that becomes apparent in the modern universe. When one contrasts *Hamlet* with *Oedipus Tyrannus* or *Othello* with *Ajax*, it quickly becomes clear that the sense of what constitutes the tragedy has dramatically changed with the birth of modernity. Shakespeare's tragic heroes evince a self-division that the single-minded heroes of Sophocles do not. In Shakespeare's modern universe, one cannot simply do one's duty to the unwritten law of the gods as Antigone does. Instead, one must question what one must do no matter what authority commands it. There are clear oppositions in the world of Sophocles, but there are internal contradictions in the universe of Shakespeare. He stands at the beginning of the modern epoch as a beacon showing that alienation is not a situation to be overcome but rather the basis for freedom.

Shakespeare's investment in alienation is most evident in *Hamlet*, the first of the great tragedies. Hamlet is a figure of self-doubt and self-critique. His division from himself stands out and enables his distance from the dictates of the social order. Toward the beginning of the play, he receives an order from his dead father, the ultimate figure of symbolic authority.[14] But rather than embark straightaway on carrying out the dead king's command to kill the usurper Claudius, Hamlet questions the source of the order, how properly to obey if the authority is legitimate, and his own status as a royal son. The ancient hero Antigone knows what she must do — bury her brother Polynices despite the ruler Creon prohibiting this act under penalty of death — and quickly does it.[15] Hamlet, in contrast, relates to his duty and to himself from a distance.

Hamlet's alienation is the source of his refusal to act

promptly and slay Claudius immediately. All the critical energy caught up in solving the problem of Hamlet's inaction fails to recognize self-doubt and self-questioning as the modern forms of action. We should not see them as inaction but rather as ways to act. No matter how convincing we might find a certain explanation of Hamlet's delay, conceiving of the play in terms of a delay misses how the alienated subject acts.[16] It doesn't act through self-certainty but through a self-laceration that divides the subject from its social situation just as it divides it from itself.[17] Hamlet is the modern subject because he acts by questioning the figure of symbolic authority as well as his own identity, which receives its support from this figure.

Toward the beginning of the play, Hamlet expresses both his own alienation and the generalized alienation of the world in which he exists. The play articulates this with reference to a temporality that no longer appears to operate as it should. Hamlet states, "The time is out of joint. O cursed spite, / That ever I was born to set it right."[18] In one sense, Hamlet refers here to the disorder that Claudius unleashes when he kills Hamlet's father and marries his mother. The world is out of joint for him specifically. But in another sense, Hamlet speaks for the modern subject as such. There is no modern subject for whom time is not out of joint: the homelessness of universal alienation becomes evident for everyone, not just for those with murdered fathers. Although Hamlet talks here about setting time right, his actions indicate that he does not believe in restoring a premodern sense of place. At no point in the play does Hamlet abandon the act of questioning that defines his modern subjectivity. His salient characteristic is his defiance of the authority of tradition, an authority that those who flee their alienation seek as a refuge.

The subject receives its orders from tradition, just as the

ghost of Hamlet's father commands Hamlet to avenge his death by killing his murderer, Claudius. But the modern subject, in contrast to the subject ensconced in tradition, can respond with doubt rather than with obedience. Rather than trust the figure of paternal authority, Hamlet questions this authority, and his response leads to further questions about the significance of existence itself. The defiance of traditional authority produces a cascading series of doubts that transform Hamlet into an exemplar of subjectivity. The articulation of a question at the site where tradition demands obedience reveals the gap in which subjectivity exists. Hamlet cannot respond to his father's demand in the way that he should because he already senses that he doesn't fully belong to the world of his father. His questioning evinces his alienation from the world in which he exists.

Hamlet's incessant questioning defines his rejection of the authority of the paternal injunction. He questions in lieu of obeying, and this questioning signals his allegiance to modernity. Shakespeare never shows Hamlet rediscovering a place within tradition during the play. Instead, he sticks out as a figure alienated from the tradition that attempts to give him a clearly defined place. His questioning does not preclude ultimately acting. When Hamlet does act and kills Claudius, Shakespeare does not present this act as the fulfillment of the destiny that his father gave to him, which is why the ghost of Hamlet's father is nowhere to be seen before, during, or after the death of Claudius. When it comes finally to killing Claudius, it is entirely Hamlet's act, because his questioning divorces this act from the authority that initially commands it. He acts without relying on any authority, but he does act rather than just content himself with rebellion, because Shakespeare understands that alienation requires that the subject take responsibility for its own actions. Hamlet cannot turn questioning into its own form of symbolic identity as so many do when they challenge figures of authority. The absence of Hamlet's father while Hamlet accomplishes the act makes clear that Shakespeare never abandoned the break that he inaugurated in the play.[19] We never return from the alienated subject of modernity to the assurances of traditional authority.

The enduring popularity of *Hamlet* derives from its status as the exemplary modern work. Although people throughout modernity attempt to retreat into a symbolic identity, in *Hamlet* Shakespeare shows the impossibility of finding any solace there. The attempt to do so always fails, as Hamlet's demeanor relative to the other characters in the play reveals. Hamlet's refusal to rely on his symbolic identity as a basis for acting offers a paradigm for modernity that simultaneously exposes the failure of any such investment. The modern subject can try to invest itself in symbolic identity, but Hamlet shows why this is not going to work out.

There are two figures who highlight alienated subjectivity in *Othello* — Othello and Iago. Neither of these figures stays where the social order places them. Neither fits within an assigned symbolic identity. Both use signification to challenge their social position, even though they seem completely opposed to each other. Othello acts with integrity to defend the established order, while Iago works diligently to upend it. But their trajectories overlap through their shared defiance of place, their shared expression of the subject's alienation.

As a military leader, Othello upholds the structure of Venetian society. But while prosecuting the interests of this society, he ends up frequenting the houses of the society's elites, including that of Brabantio. This leads to a romance between Othello and Brabantio's daughter Desdemona, a romance that challenges the racist proclivities of the society that Othello defends. As a Moor, Othello doesn't appear as a proper son-in-law in Brabantio's eyes. This romance works against Othello's own interests by putting him at odds with the society he defends as a military leader. His love for Desdemona augments Othello's alienation from his society and from himself. It ultimately portends his self-destruction after he kills her for an imagined infidelity.

The play's villain, Iago, leads Othello to self-destruction by taking advantage of Othello's alienated status. The play involves Iago persuading Othello that Desdemona is having an affair with Michael Cassio. Because he knows that he does not fit in the social order, Othello becomes susceptible to Iago's appeals to his jealousy about Desdemona and Cassio, even though they are not romantically involved with each other. Iago's awareness of Othello's alienation gives him the upper hand over Othello, who never suspects Iago of duplicity because Iago proclaims himself to be honest. Iago grasps how alienation structures subjectivity and relations between people. He uses this knowledge to destroy the relationship between Othello and Desdemona.

The appeal of Iago as a character derives from his insight into successful deception. He plants the seeds of doubt about Desdemona within Othello while at the same time proclaiming that there is nothing suspicious going on. This double gesture works perfectly on Othello due to his naïveté about the effects of signification. Iago states, "When devils will the blackest sins put on, / They do suggest at first with heavenly shows, / As I do now."[20] Othello doesn't catch on to Iago's duplicity until after he kills Desdemona for something she didn't do.

But in his final speech he demonstrates that he dies with an awareness of his alienation that had hitherto escaped him.

At the end of his life, Othello relates to himself from a distance. He has absolute loathing for himself. The subject that permits Iago to deceive him and betrays his love for Desdemona is a subject that merits only contempt. Othello kills this subject by killing himself. As he does so, he proclaims, "I took by th' throat the circumcised dog / And smote him — thus."[21] This is Othello's moment of self-transcendence, a transcendence that alienation makes possible. In smiting himself, Othello reveals that he grasps the ramifications of his self-division in a way that he hasn't before. At the end of the play, he finally embraces his status as an alienated subject. The play emphasizes the embrace of alienation as the foundation of modern subjectivity in Othello's final characterization of himself.

In contrast with Othello, Iago has a clear awareness of alienated subjectivity. He knows that signification necessarily distorts what we say, that our actions are always misperceived, and that no one can overcome self-division. And yet, he takes up this insight in the service of evil rather than ethics or political emancipation. His evil does not result from a failure to take alienation into account but rather from integrating the inescapability of alienation into his conception of subjectivity. The figure of Iago represents an omnipresent possibility in modernity. Awareness of alienation doesn't only open the possibility for emancipation. It also creates the ground — or the lack of ground — for unspeakable evil.

Iago's evil is not banal.[22] He does not instrumentalize his evil acts, using them to achieve some larger aim. Iago is a figure of diabolical evil, someone who performs evil not to accomplish some hidden interest but just for its own sake. Diabolical evil is evil done because the act of doing it brings satisfaction. In the case of diabolical evil, as Kant would have it, the subject has "an absolutely evil will" and makes "resistance to the law" its reason for acting as it does.[23] The subject of diabolical evil enjoys being evil, which is exactly what one could say about Iago.

Although he brings up diabolical evil as a theoretical possibility, Kant quickly dismisses it as an impossible position for the subject to take up. He doesn't believe that a subject can will evil for its own sake. As Kant sees it, there is radical evil — trying to do good for the wrong reasons — but there is no diabolical evil — not trying to do good at all. It's clear that Kant's insight into moral philosophy suffers from his not having read *Othello* or met Hannibal Lecter. Through the character of Iago, Shakespeare offers a convincing portrait of someone adopting an evil will. This is a possibility that exists as a result of the subject's alienation. Kant's dismissal of this possibility leads him to miss how diabolical evil helps to clarify moral action and political emancipation.[24]

Because Iago achieves the heights of diabolical evil, he reveals the limitations of this position relative to that of emancipation. In contrast to the emancipatory position, there is a clear absence of freedom in what Iago does. His actions require placing Michael Cassio and Othello in the position of enemies opposed to him. Iago needs enemies to undermine, a fact that contrasts his activity with the freedom of emancipation, which does without them. Emancipation takes universal alienation as its point of departure and sees its own self-division in that of the other. For this reason, it doesn't require enemies. Iago's diabolical evil cannot go this far and thus remains stuck in unfreedom. He doesn't reach the heights that Cordelia does in *King Lear*.

It is Lear, not Hamlet, who is Shakespeare's ultimate figure of indecision. At the beginning of *King Lear*, Lear expresses a wish to step outside of alienated subjectivity and enjoy a comfortable retirement. The problem is that there is no such thing as a comfortable retirement for the subject. No matter how earnestly one attempts to withdraw from the problems of existence (or the intrigue of the kingdom, in the case of Lear), one finds oneself inevitably involved. The subject's self-division results in its engagement with the world, an engagement that survives all efforts at retirement.[25] *King Lear* is a play about the impossibility of escaping one's alienation through an act of withdrawal.

In the first act of the play, Lear takes leave of running the kingdom, passing the authority over to his daughters. To decide how to divide the kingdom, he asks each daughter to tell him how much they love him. The opening sets up a contest of flattery, but the game is fixed from the beginning. Lear has a clear favorite, Cordelia, on whom he plans to bestow the greatest share. But the contest doesn't come off in the way that he expects.

Lear fails to understand that he and his interlocutors are all subjects of language — and thus alienated from what they say. When he demands expressions of love from each of his daughters, he receives sycophancy from his two disingenuous daughters, Goneril and Regan. Cordelia, who genuinely loves him, recognizes that subjects cannot express themselves directly, especially on command in front of a crowd. Her response disappoints Lear because it avoids the rhetorical flourish of her sisters.

While Lear suffers from failing to recognize the alienated status of subjectivity, Cordelia evinces a profound awareness of it. She shows her love for Lear specifically by not turning this love into a performance. The indirection of her speech is requisite given the alienation of her subjectivity within signification. She tells her father, "What shall Cordelia speak? Love, and be silent."[26] When Lear reproves Cordelia for her lack of expressiveness, she doubles down on her refusal to make a direct statement. Cordelia continues, "Unhappy that I am, I cannot heave / My heart into my mouth. I love your Majesty / According to my bond, no more nor less."[27] It is Cordelia's alienation — and her understanding of herself as an alienated subject — that prevents her from heaving her heart into her mouth and speaking like her sisters do.

Cordelia's refusal to betray her alienation and present herself as identical with her symbolic status makes her the hero of *King Lear*. She refuses to act as if she can be reduced to the position of daughter as her sisters do. Her alienated subjectivity gets in the way of her ability to play the part that her father demands of her. Although the play concludes with the reconciliation of Lear with the one daughter who genuinely loves him, both Lear and Cordelia die just after this reconciliation. Lear's reluctance to accept the necessity of his alienation and that of the family dooms him to ending his life ostracized. Through the negative example of Lear, the play shows the damage that the flight from alienation brings about. Cordelia's ethical being, in contrast, stems from her steadfast embrace of her alienated subjectivity.

In each of these tragedies, the irreducibility of the subject to what conditions it becomes starkly evident. The subjects of these tragedies stick out from their situations. From Hamlet's questioning of the dead father to Lear's inability to pass easily into retirement, Shakespeare's heroes evince the subject's alienation. In both cases the subjects' distance from themselves and from their society is clear. Shakespeare's tragedies point in the direction of emancipation by highlighting the inescapability of alienation.

"I Think Where I Am Not"

René Descartes accomplishes in philosophy what Shakespeare does on the stage. Even though he doesn't employ the terms *subject* or *alienation*, he is the first philosopher of the alienated subject. This makes him the inaugural philosopher of modernity. Modernity for Descartes implies a refusal of the authority of tradition, an alienation from the inherited philosophical tradition. This alienation doesn't hamper thinking but enables it to take a new tack.[28]

Descartes famously opts to begin his philosophical project with his own experience and questions about this experience rather than with the debates that he inherits from the scholastic tradition. He foregrounds his alienation from tradition in his *Discourse on the Method*, claiming to think for himself rather than to rely on any philosophical antecedents. He writes, "For it seemed to me that much more truth could be found in the reasonings which a man makes concerning matters that concern him than in those which some scholar makes in his study about speculative matters."[29] By thinking instead of studying, Descartes takes up a negative position relative to received wisdom and develops his philosophy by relating to tradition as something alien.

The method that Descartes propounds involves the negation of all prior certitude and the assertion of a fundamental doubt. Like the fictional Hamlet before him, Descartes commits himself to a project of radical questioning, a project that takes up an alien relation relative to all certainties that tradition communicates to him. Not only does Descartes abandon reading the texts of learned philosophers, he also decides to formulate his philosophy on the basis of the rejection of everything that his society holds true. This is the first modern philosophical expression of subjectivity, which emerges through a radical rejection of the conditions that would constitute it. Being a subject, as Descartes conceives it, involves kicking out the ladder on which one stands and thereby existing as if suspended in midair without anything holding one in place or protecting against one's fall. The subject is alienated from everything.

This alienation extends to the subject's relation with itself. The project of radical doubt that Descartes describes in *Meditations on First Philosophy* is a struggle against his own self-deception. This struggle demands adopting an alien relationship to oneself. In the *Meditations*, he writes, "Some years ago I was struck by the large number of falsehoods that I had accepted as true in my childhood, and by the highly doubtful nature of the whole edifice that I had subsequently based on them. I realized that it was necessary, once in the course of my life, to demolish everything completely and start again from the foundations."[30] These falsehoods have dictated Descartes' thinking, but he has the ability to suspend their effects and challenge their authority over him. This is possible only because the subject is not fully determined by its situation.

The radical alienation of the subject in Descartes' philosophy becomes clear in a classic joke about him drinking in a bar. After a few rounds, the bartender comes over to Descartes and asks, "Would you like another?" Descartes responds, "I think not," and disappears. Because he associates his existence with the thinking subject, the moment he ceases to think, he no longer exists. This joke plays on the role that the act of thinking as a proof of the subject's existence has in Descartes' philosophy, but it also reveals the disjunction between the subject and its place. Although Descartes is drinking in the bar, he is always elsewhere insofar as he is a thinking subject. He is always able to subtract himself from his situation, even if he can't make himself disappear as he does in the joke.

The freedom that the subject has from its conditions is its defining characteristic. This freedom depends on the subject's alienation from any place. Descartes sees a direct throughline from the subject's freedom from authority to its equality with other subjects, no matter where they are. The freedom of the subject from its context is a freedom that all subjects partake in equally. Hierarchy depends on context, and subjectivity, as Descartes conceives it, is the alienation from one's context. To be a subject is to belong to no place and to be at home nowhere.

His theoretical irreducibility to any particular place makes Descartes the paradigmatic modern philosopher. This attitude toward place shapes how he considers different peoples. Descartes considers that the attitudes and habits that one acquires depend entirely on the location where one is born and the context in which one grows up. As a result, one's attitudes and habits have nothing to do with one's subjectivity, although they compose one's symbolic identity. That is, if a German had grown up since infancy in China, to use Descartes' own example, she or he would act like others from China and not like a German. For Descartes, this follows from the absolute freedom of the subject, because attitude and habits have no inherent connection to the subject itself. Through the subject's ability "to abandon all the opinions [it] has hitherto accepted," the subject evinces its negative relationship to the context that gives birth to it.[31] While we like to identify Descartes as a paradigmatic figure of Western arrogance and indifference toward otherness, his conception of the alienation inherent in subjectivity enables him to articulate an early version of multicultural egalitarianism.

Perhaps the most significant break from tradition that Descartes evinces in *Discourse on the Method* resides in his decision to write in the vernacular rather than in Latin, the language of all scholastic philosophy. The very existence of the original French version of his text marks his assertion of subjectivity as the rejection of traditional authority. When he wrote a major philosophical work in French — an almost unprecedented act at the time — Descartes indicated that his audience was not confined to the educated class but included the entire literate public. Just as the subject is alienated from the context that conditions its emergence, his text is alienated from the scholastic tradition that stands behind it.

Descartes' embrace of alienation doesn't just manifest itself in his works. As befits the first modern philosopher, he lived an itinerant life, leaving France for the first time at age twenty-two and spending more than half of his adult life abroad. Responding to an invitation from Queen Christina, Descartes reluctantly visited Sweden in his early fifties and died there in 1650. Not having a place ultimately killed Descartes (as the cold in Sweden contributed to his early demise), but it was also what fueled his thinking. It is what he has in common with Shakespeare.

Modernity's Traitors

The modern break does not occur without incurring

significant resistance. The most visible forms of resistance to modernity come in the form of the champions of tradition, those who defend an identity rooted in a particular place. Such figures don't see modernity as uncovering an alienation that has always furtively existed. Instead, they blame the modern universe for imposing alienation on people and displacing them from where they could authentically dwell. Sometimes they respond to modernity with terror, sometimes with the installation of theocratic regimes, and sometimes with genocidal projects. But in every case, they tout a return to tradition as the only way to counteract the ills that modernity unleashes.

The call for a return to tradition in modernity is almost always disingenuous. The proponents of traditional values want these values without sacrificing the technological advances of modernity. In this sense, they fail to think dialectically about the era they attack. They don't see that the evils of modernity are intimately linked to its achievements. This failure is what allows them to remain comfortable in their reactionary rejection of the modern.

The reactionary critics of modernity make alienation from place the primary basis for their attack. This is certainly the case for Martin Heidegger, whose philosophy is in large part a call for the recovery of what modernity has eliminated. Heidegger provides a compelling articulation of the traditionalist view by rooting it in the specificity of place. Modernity homogenizes all places, so that it becomes impossible to dwell in one's own distinctive place. Heidegger links dwelling or being at home in a place with the form of being that mortals must take up. Our locatedness in a place attests to our finitude, which is why Heidegger values it. And yet, this becomes increasingly difficult in modernity. According to Heidegger, modernity deceives us into investing ourselves in the infinite and blinding ourselves to the finitude that defines our being. To lose our place is to lose touch with our finitude.

The chief form of failing to grasp our finitude, according to Heidegger, is the modern tendency to think of ourselves as subjects. The subject is a being without a place. Whereas Kant began to utilize the term *subject* to stress our disjointedness relative to the world, Heidegger rejects it to highlight our fundamental belonging to the world. Although many commentators note Heidegger's conspicuous rejection of the term *subject*, none emphasize how this is crucial to his antimodern philosophy and to his rejection of the heritage of German Idealism, which takes subjectivity as its starting point.[32] Heidegger must get rid of the subject because, to his sensibility, it reeks of modernity.

Rather than talk in terms of the subject, Heidegger employs the word *Dasein* to refer to beings with the capacity for self-interrogation. He refuses to refer to subjectivity precisely for the reason that Kant and Hegel insist on it: it suggests an entity separate from its world. Dasein, in contrast, connotes a being-in-the-world, a being that one cannot divorce from the world that accompanies it. Heidegger plays on two distinct senses of the term Dasein. Typically, it means "existence," but the two parts of the word, *da* and *sein*, mean "there" and "being." To think in terms of Dasein is to consider this entity as placed in a world, as existing through its dwelling in the world.

Heidegger's most sustained critique of the subject occurs in *Being and Time*, where he contrasts two opposed attitudes toward existence. When we treat objects as ready-to-hand (*zuhanden*), we view them from the perspective of experience, as objects that we use. But when we think of objects as present-at-hand (*vorhanden*), we consider them as theoretical entities that exist apart from our practical relation to them. Heidegger writes *Being and Time* in an effort to challenge the philosophical priority of thinking in terms of what is present-at-hand. He rejects a theoretical approach to the world as fundamentally misleading.

Referring to Dasein as a subject has the effect of turning it into a present-at-hand entity. As he puts it in *Being and Time*, "To define the 'I' ontologically as '*subject*' means to regard it as something always present-at-hand."[33] This is, from Heidegger's perspective, about the worst thing that one could do. In doing so, one transforms the engaged and worldly Dasein into a distant and worldless thing. Subjectivity is the name for a retreat from engagement with the world. It is the redoubt of those philosophers who cannot handle existence.

Just as Heidegger rejects talk of the subject, he also avoids discussing alienation. Given his commitment to the idea of Dasein as an entity thrown into the world, one would think that Heidegger would talk of alienation much more — and much more positively — than he does. What Heidegger calls Dasein's thrownness in the world makes it impossible for Dasein to master its world, the objects within it, or itself. Dasein never stands above or outside its world but is always in the mix.

Heidegger's criticism of modernity focuses on the illusion of mastery that it promulgates, a mastery that he associates with the idea of subjectivity. In the modern universe, we lose touch with our finitude and come to believe that there is nothing that we cannot subjugate. For Heidegger, however, we cannot even be masters of ourselves. In *Kant and the Problem of Metaphysics*, he states, "Depending upon the being which he is not, man is at the same time not master of the being which he himself is."[34] Heidegger's insistence that the human cannot master itself seems to align with a conception of alienated subjectivity, but he doesn't take his thinking in this direction. Although he takes a critical position relative to human mastery, Heidegger wrongly associates this mastery with subjectivity and the modern displacement of the human. As he sees it, we can be true to our lack of mastery only by dwelling in our proper place, not through alienation.

On the limited occasions when Heidegger does mention alienation, he does so to criticize our alienation from the world. For him, alienation is never a site of emancipation from place but bespeaks a lamentable distance from our place. The task of thinking is to facilitate a return to place, to find a way to overcome an alienating modernity.

In *Being and Time*, Heidegger associates alienation with Dasein's fall into inauthenticity. Alienation, as Heidegger uses the term, implies losing what is most ourselves. As he puts it, "When Dasein, tranquilized, and 'understanding' everything, thus compares itself with everything, it drifts along towards an alienation [*Entfremdung*] in which its ownmost potentiality-for-Being is hidden from it. Falling Being-in-the-world is not only tempting and tranquilizing; it is at the same time *alienating*."[35] In Heidegger's lingo, our fallenness into the tranquility of everydayness is alienating. Like many on the left, Heidegger criticizes modern alienation, but whereas leftists locate the cause of this alienation in the capitalist economy, Heidegger identifies it with modern science and modernity as a whole.

Heidegger's philosophical project focuses on a rediscovery of finitude and of place, a rediscovery that would counter our modern alienation. As he sees it, a return to place holds the key for recovering our sense of how we can dwell in the world. The uniformity of modern buildings makes dwelling impossible. It gives us no way to locate ourselves because it strips away the specificity of place: a modern building in Freiburg looks the same as a modern building in Jakarta. People inhabit modern buildings, but they cannot dwell in them. When one is in a modern building, one forgets its place. These buildings are alien vessels inadequate to Dasein and its being-in-the-world.[36] Modernity gives us no place to be.

Although many antimoderns are not fully versed in Heidegger's relatively arcane philosophy, he gives a theoretical voice that adroitly captures the critical lens that underlies the antimodern position. Nazism, a political position that famously attracted Heidegger's interest, promised a return to *Blut und Boden* ("blood and soil"). While Heidegger's philosophy is indifferent to blood, soil is the key to the sense of place for him. The being of Dasein is always a being rooted in the soil, a rootedness that modernity threatens, in Heidegger's eyes. Nazism spoke to him through its promise to arrest the modern obfuscation of our being-in-the-world and create a place to dwell.[37]

Very few Nazis read Heidegger, and, to his chagrin, he did not have an illustrious career as a Nazi philosopher. And yet, the same antimodern impulse that motivates Heidegger is what motivates Nazism, as well as all the other reactionary political philosophies that have emerged in the modern epoch. Heidegger lays out the theory that informs these political movements because he is the great philosopher of antimodernity, of the attempt to affirm place in the world against the modern universe's uprooting from place.[38]

Modernity creates its own reactionaries — those who reject the glimpse of our alienation that it unearths. The reactionary refusal of modernity's uprooting often seduces adherents through its promise to overcome alienation. But alienation is not the fruit of the modern revolution. It inheres in all subjectivity, which is why the reactionary return to emplacement always comes up short. There is no place to return to, not because modernity has destroyed it, but because there never was a place for the subject to begin with.

Homeward Unbound

If we search for somewhere where we will finally belong, we will inevitably fall victim to the lure of a reactionary program that promotes the nation, ethnic community, or religious group as a place where we can be at home. Emancipation always works in the other direction. There is only an uprooted emancipation in which one constantly confronts not, as Heidegger would have it, the problem of dwelling, but the inevitability of one's alienation from where one is.

If we examine two different science-fiction works, this contrast will become clearer. The updated *Battlestar Galactica* television series, which ran from 2004 to 2009, received great acclaim for its political daring.[39] It illustrates the confrontation between humans from distant worlds and the Cylons, a group of machines that want to annihilate the humans and install themselves as the dominant force in their part of the galaxy. At the beginning of the show, the Cylons launch a surprise attack that destroys almost all the humans, except for a few ships and one warship, the eponymous *Battlestar Galactica*. In the aftermath of the attack, the warship leads the other assorted vessels away from the destroyed colonies and protects them from the Cylons during their journey. The surviving humans seek what they call a lost colony, Earth, where they hope to make a new home.[40]

In the fourth and final season, after many travails and losses, the humans finally arrive at Earth. But rather than discovering a new home where they can resettle, they find a world of lifeless radioactive ruins destroyed by war. It seems as if the humans will have to learn to live without a home. However, thank God, this is just the midpoint of the season. The search goes on, and the humans end up on a much more habitable planet that they themselves christen *Earth*. Here, not only do they finally feel at home, but they settle down and establish themselves as the ancestors of the humans who populate Earth today. The series concludes with their arrival at a home, even if this isn't where they originally intended to go. The humans find a place where they belong and where they can play a foundational role in the development of intelligent life. The wager of *Battlestar Galactica* is that we should go to whatever ends necessary to find ourselves a place where we can be at home.[41]

The emphasis on finding a home establishes *Battlestar Galactica* ultimately as an antimodern work. Had the series ended with the discovery of the destroyed Earth, the result would have been far different. This would have conveyed the nonexistence of home and the necessity of embracing our alienation. But the concluding episodes of the series upend this possibility and turn the series toward the political position of Martin Heidegger.

The film *Dark City* (Alex Proyas, 1998) appeared to much less acclaim than *Battlestar Galactica*. It came and went from the cinema in 1998 with only a few spectators noticing. *Dark City* depicts a group of aliens (known as the Strangers) who manipulate the inhabitants of a city by remaking the city and changing the identities of the inhabitants every night. In the world of the film, someone can go to bed poor and alone in a shoddy apartment and wake up rich with a family in a luxurious mansion. The film's mise-en-scène makes it clear that everyone's identity is nothing but a product of external manipulation. The Strangers perform this activity in search of the human soul, what makes the individual human unique. There is one character, John Murdoch (Rufus Sewell), who sees through the manipulation because he wakes up as the transformation is occurring. It turns out that Murdoch also has the ability to manipulate reality in the way that the Strangers do, which makes it possible for him to challenge their power over the city. But throughout most of the film, he doesn't dream of challenging them. Instead, he fantasizes about escaping the dreary city that the Strangers control to what he believes to be his childhood home, Shell Beach. The fantasy of returning home to escape the horrors of modern life renders him a docile subject.

At the end of the film, Murdoch finally manages to escape the city and travel to where he imagines Shell Beach to be. He breaks open the wall at the end of the tunnel that blocks his path and uncovers that there is no Shell Beach at all. There is just a hole in the wall that opens out to the vastness of space. The film reveals that Murdoch's home is purely imaginary and that the world of the film is not tied to any place at all, not even a solar system, but is just all alone, careening through space.

Armed with this insight, Murdoch doesn't retreat into despair but revolts against the Strangers and, after defeating them, rearranges the world of the film. The political vision of *Dark City* reveals that there is no home to go back to. The only political option is to embrace one's uprootedness, to view one's alienation from a home as emancipatory. Murdoch cannot return the people of the city to their home because it has been irretrievably lost. They are condemned to spend their lives drifting through space without even being able to seek a home. But this is the condition of their freedom. Once Murdoch gives up the idea of returning home to Shell Beach, he is able to free both himself and everyone else suffering under the dominion of the Strangers. After the defeat of the Strangers, the humans must live with their alienated subjectivity. They have no secure symbolic identity to rely on that hasn't been given to them by the Strangers. But this is emancipation from external control. As the film makes clear, freedom comes through alienation, not through its overcoming.

The lesson of *Dark City*, in contrast to that of *Battlestar Galactica*, is that displacement is inescapable. At the same time, alienation from place becomes the basis for establishing an egalitarian society outside any oppressive hierarchy. We are alienated into free and equal relations. But we miss this possibility when we commit ourselves, in the manner of *Battlestar Galactica*, to overcoming alienation and finding somewhere where we can feel at home.

Modernity brings the problem of the subject to the fore. This occasions a variety of retreats from this problem — from the path of antimodern traditionalists to that of those who refuse to see alienation as necessarily universal. All these retreats end up depriving people of the opportunity that the modern universe offers. Freedom is another word for the acceptance of alienation.

Chapter Three
The Nature of Oppression

Unseen Divisions

Modernity brings about a series of horrors, so many that it seems difficult today to vaunt the modern breakthrough without immediately adding some qualification. From racist slavery and ethnic cleansing to capitalist exploitation and the atomic bomb, the balance sheet looks pretty grim for anyone judging the modern universe.[1] While some of these were the products of antimodern reactions, they nonetheless occurred amid the modern era and under the aegis of modernity. The modern impulse has at least some culpability for the horrors that have occurred during the period that it inaugurated.

This raises the fundamental question of whether modernity is worth the price that we pay for it. Perhaps some antimodern program is in order, given modernity's unenviable record.[2] This line of thinking appears to have something to say for it when we survey the damage that modernity has done, perhaps most seriously its threat to continued human life on the planet. How we think about alienation can help us make sense of these problems that modernity has spawned. It can also assist us in thinking about whether the project of modernity is worth sustaining at all.

It might seem as if all these horrors are attributable

to the alienation that exists in the modern universe. Not coincidentally, that is how most theorists have judged them. According to the theoretical doxa, modern alienation leads to the unrelenting destruction of the natural world. It permits soldiers to slaughter ethnic groups with impunity. It encourages business owners to pry every bit of uncompensated labor out of their workers that they can. And it enables a bomber pilot to kill roughly one hundred thousand people in an instant without ever expressing a modicum of regret.[3] Those are some of modernity's exceptional achievements. Examining where modernity leads is almost enough to turn anyone into an antimodernist, just as visiting a slaughterhouse can make a vegan of even the most recalcitrant meat eater. But while it appears as if modern alienation is the culprit for all modernity's sins, a closer look tells a vastly different story.

The horrors of modernity are not the result of the alienation that it unleashes, because modernity does not generate alienated subjectivity. Even if premodern theorists didn't think of themselves as alienated subjects, they were nonetheless. Modernity makes us aware of the subject's alienation by exposing its uprootedness from place, but this uprootedness has always existed. Modernity discovers alienation; it does not invent it. The discovery of alienation is emancipatory, not oppressive. Without this discovery, subjects can only remain the prisoners of tradition. This is why the modern gambit is worth the cost.

Things go wrong in the modern epoch not because it generates alienation but because people take flight from the alienation it reveals. The collective inability to accept alienation as constitutive leads to modernity's worst sins. Oppression occurs through the refusal of alienation, the attempt to create a way of living that would escape the trauma of alienated subjectivity. Every oppressive act and every oppressive structure can be linked to an attempt to avoid confronting a fundamental alienation. The point is not that modernity remains unfinished or incomplete but that we haven't wrestled with the ramifications of the alienation that modernity has laid bare and invited us to confront. In the effort to get away from this confrontation, modern subjects have unleashed a series of unrelenting horrors. We require one more effort to be modern, not an abandonment of modernity.

In response to modernity laying our alienation bare, modern subjects have fled from this revelation into forms of barbarism unseen in the premodern world.[4] Modernity multiplies the horrors of the premodern past because it forces a confrontation with alienation that was easier to avoid in this past. The violence of capitalism, racism, and sexism — to say nothing of that of modern wars and planetary destruction — emerges in response to the perceptibility of alienation in the modern universe.[5] This violence outstrips its premodern antecedents because the threat of alienation becomes more evident. Modern subjects use violence to keep people in a particular symbolic position, to reassure themselves that everyone and everything still has a place. But modern alienation always trumps these efforts at confining subjects to their place. Modern subjects cannot put the genie of alienation back in its premodern bottle.

We have failed to see the emancipatory quality of alienation because theorists have misunderstood its structure and wrongly linked alienation to oppression. In *Dialectic of Enlightenment*, Max Horkheimer and Theodor Adorno draw a connection between modern barbarism and self-estrangement. They claim, "Human beings are so radically estranged from themselves and from nature that they know only how to use and harm each other."[6] Horkheimer and Adorno see nothing emancipatory about alienation. For them, our distance from ourselves and from others simply makes us capable of the most extreme cruelty. In their accounting, distance from ourselves — alienation — is not emancipatory.[7]

Adorno and Horkheimer fail to see that what disrupts our self-identity is not a problem that we must try to overcome but the basis for our freedom, our equality, our solidarity, and our creativity. Without alienation, we are beings reducible to our social context, imprisoned in our given form of identity. In such a situation, what is given would be completely determinative. By redeeming alienation as a force for emancipation, we can reevaluate our political struggle. The point is to recognize alienation as an attractive alternative rather than as a condition that we try to escape without any prospect of success.

This requires reconceptualizing oppression. Even though this is how we often think of it, oppression cannot be equivalent to the experience of alienation, since alienation is universal. Those who are oppressed are not fated to be alienated subjects with no possibility of overcoming their alienation. The forces of oppression do not thrust oppressed groups into an unrelenting alienation. Instead, oppression sets both the oppressing and the oppressed groups into their symbolic identities, so that everyone has a proper place. The lure of an oppressive system for the oppressor is that it will provide a definite social location for everyone, with the illusory promise that no one will continue to experience alienation. The oppressor and the oppressed become nothing more than their symbolic identities. The aim of oppression is to transform all subjectivity into self-identical entity. That said, an oppressive society is not magically composed of self-identical beings. No one escapes the divide of alienated subjectivity, not even in the most oppressive society imaginable.[8] But to be oppressed is to be positioned, pushed into an identity without a clear path to get out of it. Oppression works to make self-division invisible even as it relies on this self-division.

Most people know what oppression looks like. It is a social order that leaves a mass of people in poverty, condemns a certain group to a denigrated position relative to others, or ostracizes some for who they are. To regard someone in an oppressive way is to classify the person as a substantial entity or as a whole. It is to refuse to allow this person to exist as a divided and contradictory subject with desires that are at odds with themselves.[9] One does this to create the illusion that both oneself and the other are self-identical beings.

One indication of the existence of oppression is the reduction of a group to a collective identity with definite desires or ways of being. In the oppressed situation, all subjects become reducible to a consistent symbolic identity. Identity overwhelms subjectivity in the oppressive viewpoint, which is why people tend to identify those in an oppressed position in a collective way, with statements such as "They smell bad" or "They are lazy" or even "They are destroying our nation." One collectivizes others in this way when one refuses to recognize them as alienated from themselves and thus irreducible to any such identity.

The characterization can even be a positive one, such as "All mothers love their children." It might be difficult to recognize this statement as a sexist one since it makes an unqualified positive statement about women who have children, but its sexism consists in the attribution of an undivided symbolic identity to all childbearing women. According to the logic of this statement, women are not subjects but substantial beings. If mothers were subjects, some would love their children, but some would not. And even those who did would have times when they didn't. The alienated subject is not identical with itself but desires in contradictory ways. But the forces of oppression attempt to deny their targets the capacity for alienation. Oppression aims at making them one with themselves.

Modernity makes alienation visible, but modern subjects as a rule retreat from the visibility of alienation into the assurance of identity. Oppression in the modern universe emerges through this retreat. Even though modernity makes evident the alienation underlying every identity, oppression works to obscure this alienation, to convince subjects that there are those who can be identified with their place. The fight against this oppression and the fight to embrace universal alienation are one and the same struggle.[10]

It might appear as if the alienation of subjectivity and the alienation that capitalist society produces are different animals. But the social forms of alienation always express the fundamental alienation of subjectivity. In this sense, the ways that alienation appears in society actually make evident our fundamental alienation. These different types of alienation all reveal an internal distance within the subject, a distance between the subject and its identity, which is why they have a revelatory power. Under capitalism, for instance, my alienation from the product of my labor enables me to recognize my alienated subjectivity. This is in itself not an oppressive situation but can be emancipatory insofar as it facilitates the embrace of the fundamental alienation that defines me as a subject. But the problem is that capitalism presents alienation as a problem to overcome rather than a path to emancipation. That is the integral to its oppressiveness.

The Capitalist Future

Subjects experience alienation in capitalist society. They work to produce commodities that generate profits for others and insufficiency for themselves. They see themselves constantly on the outside of the enjoyment that others seem to be having and think that they will find their own enjoyment through whatever they don't yet have. Instead of accumulating wealth, the majority accumulate debt. But capitalism takes an ideological hold of people so tightly not because it alienates them but because it promises a cure for their alienation. Every transaction that occurs in capitalist society has the image of an end to alienation animating it.[11] Even though capitalism forces subjects to experience their alienation, it does so while also promulgating the promise of a cure for this problem. Under capitalism, alienation appears as a remediable problem, not as the structure that constitutes subjectivity. This is the key to capitalism's structure and to its attraction for even those who don't benefit materially from it.[12]

Capitalism appeals to people as desiring beings. It has a libidinal dimension that draws them in, that derives from its promise of overcoming alienation. The commodity form defines capitalist society. This form compels our interest because it connotes the coming end of alienated subjectivity. When I look at the commodity, I see the possibility of achieving plenitude. Through its detachment from the labor process or its obfuscation of the labor within it, the commodity passes itself off as a pure excess, one not besmirched by any alienation. By partaking of the commodity, one can overcome alienation and experience pure excess — or so capitalist society tells us. This holds both for the capitalist who sells it and for the consumer who buys it. One sells or buys the commodity in order to approach pure excess and escape the alienation that defines our subjectivity. Capitalism doesn't create alienation but does everything it can to convince us that there is a way to escape it.

Let's look at a simple commodity: the car. The car generates value for the capitalists who sell it. Through the sale of cars, capitalists increase their capital. In doing so, they strive toward a future of infinite accumulation, even though they will never attain this future. At the same time, those who buy cars see in them the promise of an infinite enjoyment that these commodities will provide. Advertisers convince people to buy new cars that they don't need because the new car promises an end to alienation that the current one doesn't provide. Even though buying the car never works as a cure for the alienated state, the commodity's seductive power never wanes for the capitalist subject. This suggests the extreme power that the possibility of escaping alienation has over people. Both the producer and the consumer invest themselves in the commodity for the sake of the unalienated future that it contains.

The focus on a cure for alienation generates a vast number of new commodities each year. Although the majority of these commodities fail to catch on and end up lost to history, their quantity alone evinces capitalism's commitment to proposing a cure to alienation. No one needs Diet Caffeine-Free Mountain Dew, but the existence of this commodity, just like every other commodity, helps perpetuate the fantasy of an end to alienation that constitutes the essence of capitalism's appeal. In the *Grundrisse*, Marx points out that capitalism must create needs that do not exist. He states, "Production not only supplies a material for the need, but it also supplies a need for the material."[13] This need for the material relies on the fantasy that every new commodity assists in generating. Capitalism bombards its subjects with tens of thousands of new products each year because it must constantly reinvigorate its promise of an escape from alienation. Without the barrage of novelty, we would quickly become aware of our alienated subjectivity and lose touch with the fantasy of escaping it.

Focusing on the question of alienation allows us to rethink the critique of capitalist society and how it distorts our existence. The problem with capitalism is not that it creates an alienated society but that it prevents us from recognizing our constitutive alienation. The basic structure of capitalism leads us to see alienation as a problem that has a solution rather than as the structure of our subjectivity. The would-be solution appears in the commodity.

Capitalism surrounds us with commodities and imprints the commodity form on us. It constantly holds out the solution to alienation in the commodity, which contains the promise of an end to alienated subjectivity. The fact that this never occurs doesn't detract from capitalism's power over me. Each failure further ensconces me in the logic of capitalism. The more I fail to achieve the unalienated future, the more I strive for it.

But there is an even more deleterious effect than this. When I choose one commodity over another, the other option does not disappear. Instead, it remains in force and mediates my relationship to the commodity that I have chosen. Because I have not chosen it, this other commodity harbors a potential for escaping alienation that exceeds the potential I find in the commodity I did choose. The other option contains this possibility only insofar as I relate to it as an imaginary object. Were I to obtain it, the relief from alienation it delivered would not exceed that of the commodity I did choose. It offers more plenitude only insofar as it remains unchosen.

The unchosen commodity retains the plenitude that the commodity I chose loses once I obtain it. I am thus stuck in a perpetual mode of desire for what I didn't choose because the capitalist subject always chooses wrongly. I opt for Junior Mints instead of Milk Duds, but every taste of the Junior Mints reminds me that I am not tasting Milk Duds like the person next to me at the movie theater. The moment I have a glimpse of my alienation and say to myself, "Hey, these Junior Mints aren't actually all that great," I'm able to turn away from it by considering the alternate commodity that I didn't choose, the Milk Duds. This is the psychic trap that the commodity form creates for the subject. The capitalist subject is always missing out on something better, something better that holds the promise of a cure for its alienation. We experience plenty of alienation under capitalism, but we also continually imagine its commodified remedy.

The commodity form causes us to conceptualize our possibilities without any limits. As structured by the commodity form, the only acceptable boundary is the subjectivity of the other, never an intrinsic limitation within our own subjectivity. But this idea of subjectivity is profoundly misleading. When we view subjectivity as intrinsically unlimited, or as limited only by someone else, we interpret every external barrier that we encounter as an encroachment on our own possibilities. As a result, our existence seems always to be under assault from all sides and never able to realize itself fully. We don't recognize that alienation is fundamental to our subjectivity.

Capitalism tries to convince us that our alienation is temporary and fleeting rather than constitutive of who we are.

The promise of an unalienated future leads to the widespread acceptance of a system that produces massive inequalities, social isolation, and an assault on freedom. Capitalism compensates for these deficiencies with the fantasy that it proffers. Even though no one benefits from capitalism in the way that the system promises, its seductive power is unparalleled.[14] It seduces both those who seem to succeed and many of those who fail.

The fantasy that underwrites the entire capitalist enterprise is one of overcoming alienation through accumulation. The capitalist's rapaciousness stems directly from the centrality of this fantasy and would dissipate without it. Capitalism is a practice, but the mindless accumulation required to sustain it is impossible without the prospect of healing the wound of alienation that animates it. There is no capitalist universe in which one can accept alienation as a fact of existence. That is the key to its oppressiveness. The way to fight it is to insist on the truth of the moments of alienation that it exposes, to remain disappointed with one's Junior Mints without any hope for relief from Milk Duds.

Race to the Bottom

Racism is a modern invention. Although hatred between different peoples predates modernity, the specificity of racism belongs to the modern epoch. Prior to modernity, subjects identified themselves as various peoples and came together in different groups, but there was no such thing as racial difference. The modern invention of race underlies and makes possible slavery, colonialism, systematic oppression, widespread theft, and the pillaging of massive territories. It is at the basis of modernity's worst crimes.[15]

Racism permits modern subjects to act in ways that violate the moral edicts that modern philosophy articulates. All the moral philosophers of modernity, no matter what their specific philosophical stripe, condemn the buying and selling of people as if they were nothing but material commodities. And yet, under the spell of racism, slave owners and traders have engaged in this activity, and most of them have still considered themselves good, moral people. This is possible because they don't believe that they are dealing with subjects when they buy and sell slaves. Racial difference indicates, for those ensconced in a racist social structure, an absence of subjectivity. Modernity compels subjects to view all other subjects as their equals, but the concept of racial difference changes that outlook. The human rights that modern society espouses count only for those who belong to this society. Those on the outside don't count.[16] They are nothing but a symbolic identity that has no status within the social order.

European racism unevenly distributes the impact of modernity. It allows some to regard themselves as modern while consigning others to a premodern status. In *The Wretched of the Earth*, Frantz Fanon sees the denigration of the racial other as the underside of modernity. He claims, "This Europe, which never stopped talking of man, which never stopped proclaiming its sole concern was man, we now know the price of suffering humanity has paid for every one of its spiritual victories."[17] As Fanon points out, the values of modernity don't apply to everyone equally. Racism enables those invested in it to see the racial other as a self-identical being that can be terrorized without compunction.

But according to the racist viewpoint, there is no subjectivity at all, even for the racists themselves. This is why it is so appealing for those invested in it. Racism avoids considering either the racist subject itself or the racial other it attacks as alienated. There are just two disparate racial identities that confront each other in a stable hierarchy. The racists know where they stand in their symbolic identity because they know where the racial other stands. Everyone has a place in the racist system.[18] If one has a race, one gains a sense of security about one's symbolic identity. Racism is a system for distributing secure positions within a symbolic world. It is a system that enables those participating in it to avoid the encounter with their own alienation and that of the other.

Racism elevates one symbolic identity by denigrating another. Those invested in the racist structure gain a sense of their own superiority, but even more important, they gain a sense of what they are. The identification of the racial other assures them of what they are by showing them what they are not. Without the Jew, the Aryan would have no identity. Without blackness, whiteness would have no value. Under the spell of racism, all these identities appear substantialized and safe from the trauma of alienated subjectivity.

The philosophical basis for racism is the denial of the racist's own alienated status and the denial of alienation in the other as well. Racism is the attempt to reject the modern discovery of universal alienation by seeking sanctuary in secure racial identities. In a racist society, identity takes the place of subjectivity. On one side, identity is idealized, while on the other, it is denigrated.[19] The divide doesn't so much separate the subject from its other as it separates one symbolic identity from another. Each of these identities functions as a path for the avoidance of alienated subjectivity. One can believe that it is possible to overcome alienation when racial identity appears to have a genuine reality.

The first task of the modern racist project is the invention of race. In order to create a race to oppress, the racist project must begin by creating distinct races. Race has no biological existence, and people have no intrinsic reason to think in terms of racial difference. But racialized thinking offers them a path out of the question of their subjectivity. For this to be successful, people must accept races as naturally existing. If they recognize race as the product of a racist act, that act will not have functioned properly. The act works only if it occurs invisibly. It is for this reason that Barbara and Karen Fields work to peel back the racist act hidden in every invocation of race as having a genuine existence.[20]

In *Racecraft*, the Fields sisters explain that the most important move that the racist project makes is to hide itself under the patina of race. If race really exists, then racism appears as its inevitable outgrowth. By transforming racism into racial difference, the racist project covers its own tracks. It turns an action that emerges in response to the subject's alienation into a question of identity. As the Fields sisters put it, "*The race-racism maneuver transforms racist action (invidious treatment) into race (inborn difference).*"[21] Racism is the act of a group of subjects, a social order, but the act disguises itself as a response to identities that exist prior to it. Racial identity then seems as if it triggers the racist subject's act, when the causality actually works the other way around. There is no racial identity prior to the racist act that produces it. There is a racist subject — and this subject's act — behind every formation of a racial identity.

The struggle against racism requires the translation of symbolic identities back into the acts of alienated subjects.

Where race appears, we must see the racist act that creates this racial difference. Racism offers subjects a way of avoiding the confrontation with alienation. To challenge racism is to thrust oneself directly into the position of the alienated subject.

This is precisely the point that Paul Gilroy takes up in *Against Race*. Gilroy sees how modernity brings with it the horror of racism, but at the same time, he recognizes that there is only a modern emancipation. He states, "A susceptibility to the appeal of authoritarian irrationalism has become part of what it means to be a modern person. It is bound to the dreams of enlightenment and autonomy as an ever-present alternative."[22] The fight against modern racism (which is the only form of racism) entails asserting universal modernity. Racism only works so long as at least one group of people does not qualify as subjects of modernity, in which case their oppressors can also view themselves through the lens of self-identity.

The exclusion of some from participation in modern existence not only consigns this group to an antimodern form of life, but it also equally allows those who consider themselves modern to indulge in the barbaric treatment of this racial other. Racism licenses antimodernity on both sides of the divide. A modernity without this antimodern supplement would be a radicalized modernity. It would be an emancipated modernity.

A Woman's Place

Like racism, sexism attempts to ensconce its targets and those invested in it in a clear symbolic identity. Under the spell of sexism, no one appears as an alienated subject. Instead, the opposition of man and woman provides two stable identities to occupy. In this opposition, both sides have a symbolic place, but the symbolic place of the women becomes especially circumscribed. Women have a place confined to the domestic sphere.[23]

According to the sexist ideology, the man goes out into the world to interact with others, while the woman occupies herself with a domestic role. The man discovers who he is through engagement with the *nomos*, while the woman remains unalienated and attends to the *oikos*. Or, as the sexist cliché has it, "A woman's place is in the home." Sexism doesn't alienate women. It treats them as if they were whole beings incapable of suffering from alienation.[24]

The feminist analysis of how sexism works reveals the role that the refusal of alienation plays in oppressive relations. We can see an instance of how oppression operates in Simone de Beauvoir's *The Second Sex*. In this work, Beauvoir describes the oppression of women throughout agrarian history as a reduction of the feminine to an image of self-identity. To be treated as a woman is to be regarded as incapable of experiencing alienation from oneself, of internalizing the universal. Beauvoir recounts the inability of women within a sexist society to recognize their alienation from their particularity. This is the sense of her statement that "woman... wallows in immanence; but first she was enclosed in it."[25] To wallow in immanence is to be what one is, to be unable to recognize oneself as alienated in one's identity. One might say that Beauvoir describes femininity as the reduction of female subjectivity to the status of a particular identity. Beauvoir is critical of sexist society for not allowing women to encounter the interruption of universality. Sexism prevents women from confronting their status as alienated subjects. That's what it means to wallow in immanence.[26]

Beauvoir relates how sexism, throughout its long history, identifies the woman with her body. To be a woman is to be fixed in a bodily identity without hope of escape. Before the woman is trapped in the domestic sphere, she becomes identical with the body itself. According to Beauvoir, this identification rules women out of sports, demanding jobs, and intellectual activities. As one trapped in the body, a woman cannot become a priest or a political leader. All of the processes associated with a woman's body — menstruation, pregnancy, menopause — become signifiers of the body that the woman cannot escape. This unavoidable embodiment serves as a justification for denigrating the feminine.

Celebrating the feminine does not make the situation any better. The embrace of the feminine can be just as oppressive as its degradation. This is the primary tenet of Betty Friedan's argument in *The Feminine Mystique*. Here, Freidan recognizes that the celebration of the feminine can only work effectively if it envisions femininity as an unalienated identity. She wrote *The Feminine Mystique* to remind women of their alienation, not to encourage them to surmount it. One can only be emancipated as an alienated subject.

According to Friedan, valuing the feminine is the primary way that sexist society oppresses women. She writes, "The feminine mystique says that the highest value and the only commitment for women is the fulfillment of their own femininity. It says that the great mistake of Western culture, through most of its history, has been the undervaluation of this femininity."[27] Friedan reacts to the attempt to place women on a pedestal. Sexism works to convince women that their identity as women gives them an intrinsic value, that what they are as women matters more than what they might do.

The aim is to convince women to accept their place in society instead of seeking to discover their alienated subjectivity.[28]

The danger of women discovering their alienation is also the central concern in Olivia Wilde's wildly underappreciated *Don't Worry Darling* (2022), one of the great diagnoses of the psychic structure of sexist oppression. This feminist masterpiece shows just how far men will go to convince women that they don't suffer from any alienation — and it illustrates how women can become seduced by this lure of an unalienated symbolic identity in which one has a place. Men will submit themselves to an extremely oppressive economic situation as long as they can ensconce the female objects of their desire in the illusion of a secure identity.

Don't Worry Darling depicts a closed world in the town of Victory, California, where the women take care of their households while their husbands spend each day working at Victory Headquarters. The idyllic town is a sexist utopia in which the women remain in their place while the men work to sustain it by earning the money to finance its upkeep. It turns out, however, that this sexist fantasy is really just a simulation created by Frank (Chris Pine), who convinced the other men to finance it.

As the main character Alice Chambers (Florence Pugh) gradually comes to an awakening and discovers that they are living in a simulation, we recognize that the men fund their participation and that of their spouses through work in the real world. When they leave for work each morning, they actually leave the simulation to work outside it. For her part, far from being a bored housewife in an isolated town, Alice is an emergency-room doctor. When we see flashbacks to this time in Alice's life, it is clear that she suffers from the alienation of this work. She is weary of the long hours and exhausting labor, but at the same time, she exhibits a satisfaction that she lacks in the simulation.

The film contrasts the comfort of Alice's symbolic identity in Victory with the alienation of her life as a doctor outside it. Even though the simulation offers her the image of wholeness, the alienated existence of her real life appears preferable, not just because it's real and not fake, but because suffering her alienation is satisfying in a way that being rooted in a place is not.

The lure of a stable identity seduces some, but oppression occasions resistance because alienation is not without its own appeal. Existing as an alienated subject gives one autonomy from external determinations. Alienation indicates that one is not identical with any symbolic identity. It signals that one can act contrary to the expectations inherent in one's identity. The fight against oppression is a fight to assert one's alienation against the oppressive enforcement of an identity. To strive to embrace one's alienated subjectivity is to be engaged in the fight against oppression of all stripes.

Chapter Four
The Dream of Overcoming

Capital Punishment

The negative press that alienation endures is not just due to its lack of a good agent or publicist. It stems directly from the theoretical success of Karl Marx and his historical triumph over Hegel as the chief philosopher for the project of emancipation. Even as Marxist regimes collapsed around the world, critics of capitalist society continued to repeat Marx's criticism of this society as an alienating one. At every moment of crisis within the capitalist economy, we hear the mantra of capitalist alienation.[1] Against Marx's idea that capitalism is alienating, Hegel argues that alienation is irreducible and therefore universal. Although capitalism alienates us, it has no monopoly on this. But no one turns to Hegel's philosophy of universal alienation as an alternative to Marx, despite the fact that he provides a way of conceiving an emancipatory political project that takes into account the irreducibility of the alienated subject. For this reason, it's worth re-examining how Hegel and Marx view the question of alienation.

When Marx envisions how his thought differs from Hegel's, he imagines that his transformation of the dialectical system will stop all the blood from rushing to Hegel's head. That is, Hegel's problem, as Marx sees it, is that he conceives of his system upside down. He makes the mistake that all philosophers make when he contends that ideas, not material conditions, move the world. While Hegel rightly sees that contradictions are the engine of history, he doesn't recognize that this task falls to material contradictions, not ideal ones. Hegel's is a dialectic that moves in precisely the wrong direction — from idea to materiality. Marx aims to provide a corrective, to flip Hegel on his feet and thereby solve his circulatory problems by highlighting the priority of material relations over ideas.

In his 1873 postface to the second edition of *Capital*, Marx lays out this oft-cited argument. Critics are so taken by Marx's claim because it brings Hegel's philosophy down to earth and reveals the economic nitty-gritty that really drives our existence. According to this line of thought, Hegel's error consists in believing that ideas trump matter.[2] In contrast with Hegel, Marx proposes marrying the dialectical method to the empirical realities within which we exist. He writes, "The mystification which the dialectic suffers in Hegel's hands by no means prevents him from being the first to present its general forms of motion in a comprehensive and conscious manner. With him it is standing on its head. It must be inverted, in order to discover the rational kernel within the mystical shell."[3] Marx envisions this inversion as the essential core of his transformation of the Hegelian system. Marx sees himself as offering a radical corrective that will turn Hegel's philosophical system into a theory organized toward political action.[4] A philosophy that loudly proclaims it cannot change the world becomes a political theory whose only goal is to do so.[5]

But what Marx, along with most of those commenting on this relationship, misses is the extent to which he also departs from Hegel on a much more crucial question — that of alienation.

Marx's view that capitalism alienates workers from the products of their labor and that communism represents a cure for this alienation plays a determinative role for the political movements that take up the mantle of his thought. Marxism's champions proffer it as a response to alienated capitalist life. Even more than this, other leftist political movements — those not explicitly associated with Marx — take their lead from Marx's critique of alienation and present their program as an answer to alienation. Highlighting alienation as a problem that politics must solve is Marx's innovation, one that marks a retreat from Hegel's understanding of alienation.

Hegel grants alienation a positive role in the development of subjectivity that Marx will subsequently write out of his own dialectical system. Hegel is the philosopher of alienation, the one who recognizes that alienation is not a misfortune that besets the subject. It is not a problem to be overcome but the site of freedom and the basis for equality. As Hegel grasps, there is no subjectivity at all without alienation. As he puts it in the *Phenomenology of Spirit*, "Self-consciousness is only *something*, it only has *reality* insofar as it alienates itself from itself."[6] As it separates the subject from itself, alienation makes possible the mediated self-relation that defines subjectivity. Whatever terms he uses for it — *Entfremdung* or *Entäußerung* in German — Hegel never conceives of alienation critically. There is no point in all his writing and lectures when he criticizes alienation.

For Hegel, alienation is positive because it delivers us from the stasis of self-identity. Through alienation, the subject enters into what is other than itself and becomes who it is as it transforms into what it isn't. Alienation rips us out of our natural being and generates subjectivity.[7] Hegel theorizes the subject as an entity that must find itself at home in what is absolutely other to it, and this can only occur through a process of alienation. Dialectics is, for Hegel, a system in which there is no respite from alienation, in which alienation is total.[8]

Hegel's dialectical method operates by recognizing the alien within what purports to be identical with itself. Let's look at a simple proposition, such as "Venus is the evening star." This is a statement of identity rather than of predication, since the evening star is identical to Venus. It is not a quality that Venus has. Regarded in a nondialectical way, this proposition bespeaks identity without a trace of difference: Venus and the evening star are the same thing. But according to Hegel, even straightforward statements of identity cannot avoid revealing the alien within the identical. The act of identifying Venus and the evening star indicates that Venus is not a self-identical entity. It can be equated with itself (as the evening star) because it is not impervious to what it is not. Identity emerges through its relations, not by isolating itself from everything that is different. This means that every identity involves contradictions.

Dialectics is the exploration of the contradictions that inhere within every identity. Whatever seems identical is ultimately revealed, through a dialectical interpretation, as self-divided and involved in what is other to it. For Hegel, contradiction is ontological, and alienation is the way that contradiction manifests itself in the subject. The subject attains freedom through the alienation that generates and sustains subjectivity. Hegel pursues a dialectical interpretation of the subject to bring out the emancipatory power of its alienation.[9]

As a result, one could say that Marx's most radical break from Hegel consists in his critique of alienation and his investment in its overcoming. This is also the point at which Marx opens a fraught theoretical path. Once one embarks on the project of overcoming alienation, one dooms oneself to an unending — and losing — struggle, a losing struggle bent on ultimately winning. This perspective also leads us to look at political struggles in a misleading way. Alienation is not a trap to escape but the self-distancing that provides the basis for freedom.

In Marx's early writings, alienation plays a major role. As he sees it, alienation is precisely the damage that capitalist society does to us.[10] One of the most widely accepted claims from Marx's critique of capitalism is that this economic system creates an alienated society. For Marx, the principal form that alienation takes in capitalism is that workers become alienated from the products of their labor.[11] When a worker produces a commodity, the capitalist owns this commodity and sells it for a profit, thereby creating an insurmountable gulf between the two. Rather than having the product to do with what they will, workers must confront what they produce in the alien form of the commodity, which they must buy for themselves if they want to have it. The capitalist owns and profits from what the workers create. This alienation is far from salutary — and thus far from Hegel's conception of how alienation functions.

Whereas in feudal society artisans produced goods through a holistic process that relied on their specialized knowledge and from which they directly reaped the benefits, the working class laboring under capitalist relations of production loses this relationship to the products of its labor. The division of labor eliminates the know-how of the feudal artisan, while the capitalist, not the worker, profits from the sale of the commodity. The artisan's goods become the capitalist's commodities, and in the process, the producer's labor becomes alienated. The commodity is the name for the alienated product of labor.

As Marx formulates it in his early writings, humanity objectifies itself through productive labor. But under capitalism, we become alienated from our nature as productive beings and alienated from each other through the incessant demand for competition. Capitalism creates a collective in the form of the working class, but it doesn't allow this collective to become conscious of itself as a collective. Each worker experiences existence as isolated and solitary, as an existence alienated from the rest of the society. In the *Economic and Philosophic Manuscripts of 1844*, Marx lays out this theoretical position. He writes, "In tearing away from man the object of his production ... estranged labor tears from him his *species life*, his real objectivity as a member of the species."[12] Here, Marx points out that objectification through labor is the way that humanity knows itself, but he also contends that this is what capitalism makes impossible by alienating us from what we create and from each other. The loss of what he calls species life under capitalism is a loss of what is most essential about humanity.[13]

This critique of capitalist alienation has found a receptive audience not just among Marxists, but also with anarchists, communalists, and even some conservatives. In addition to alienating workers from the product of their labor, capitalism seems to create an alienated social life, a situation in which people relate to each other through the mediation of the commodity rather than directly. Those who call for an end to alienation want to achieve a society in which we overcome the distance between subjectivity and symbolic identity. In such a society, everyone would be recognized as who they are. There would be no gap internal to the subject or between one subject and others. Such a social order would, in Hegel's view, not only be impossible. It would also be a nightmare.

A Strange Hegel

Far from dreaming of a future free from alienation, Hegel theorizes the achievement of freedom through alienation. He is the first thinker to explicitly include alienation in his philosophy, and he conceives it in a completely positive fashion.[14] Alienation is a positive process for Hegel because it takes us away from our given situation and forces us into an encounter with what is other. Through alienation, we become who we are as we become different from what we are. Alienation allows us to recognize that what appears opposed to us is actually constitutive of who we are.

When we occupy ourselves solely with what appears immediately certain to us, we miss the forces of mediation that create this sense of immediacy. Our initial self-certainty is actually a self-deception that depends on not seeing what determines us. As we experience our alienation, however, this self-certainty dissolves. Our assurance about our identity evaporates. Subjectivity, according to Hegel, finds itself through "violence at its own hands [that] brings to ruin its own restricted satisfaction."[15] We discover the truth of our subjectivity not in what we initially take ourselves to be but in how we end up after we have enacted this violence against ourselves. This self-distancing reveals who we are in a way that our immediate certainty obscures. Alienation into the foreign frees us from the tyranny of the given.

Alienation works in Hegel's system in two moments. At first, children become alienated through education or *Bildung*. Hegel completely rejects the romantic image of an educational process that develops the intrinsic potential of the child.[16] Instead, he conceives of education as an act of violence done to the child, a violence that disrupts the child's inherent tendencies rather than allowing them to blossom according to their own logic. This is because their own logic is never that of the subject itself but rather of what invisibly determines it. The alien violence of education is what initially frees the child from its familial and social situation. In this sense, education is an emancipatory violence.[17]

Hegel emphasizes the confrontation with alien thinking that occurs in education.[18] Education forces children into an alien process. They must occupy themselves with rote learning and mechanical drills in order to acquire the ability to think for themselves. They cannot just pass directly to independent thinking but must traverse the alienating mechanical process that occurs in the first years of education. The subject capable of freedom emerges out of this alien imposition that appears to bear no resemblance to freedom. My ability to think independently depends on an initial dependence on the routinized development of skills.

After the society imposes an alienating education on the subject, Hegel believes that an additional step of alienation is necessary for the subject to attain freedom. In the second moment of alienation, the subject takes up alienation for itself. It alienates itself from its own objective situation. According to Hegel, no one is simply identical with their situation. Instead, subjects must relate to their situation as if they were foreign intruders in it.

This is evident in the most famous thing that Hegel ever wrote — the dialectic of the master and the servant. During this dialectical relation, the master realizes that mastery is illusory because of its complete dependence on the lowly servant, while the servant recognizes its freedom by grasping how the act of servitude produces autonomy. Each position becomes what is other to itself through a fundamental alienation. The alienated master finds itself to be the servant of the servant, and the alienated servant discovers that it has autonomy relative to the master through its actions.

As a result of alienation, subjectivity attains freedom. But this freedom exists in relation to the constraint of the objective situation. Hegel sees the concept of fate as a popular way of articulating the constraint that the free subject encounters. Without the alienation that separates the subject from their situation and grants them freedom, it would make no sense to talk about fate. In the *Science of Logic*, Hegel claims that alienation is the precondition for the experience of fate. He states, "Only self-consciousness has fate in a strict sense, because it is *free*, and therefore in the *singularity* of its 'I' it absolutely exists *in and for itself* and can oppose itself to its objective universality and *alienate* itself from it. By this separation, however, it excites against itself the mechanical relation of a fate."[19] Even though the mention of fate suggests unfreedom, Hegel links it to the subject's freedom. One can only experience the constraint of fate once one has alienated oneself from one's situation and attained freedom. For Hegel, we alienate ourselves into freedom after being subjected to the alienated force of education.

The different positions that Hegel and Marx have on alienation are significant because they end up producing different portraits of what society might become. For Hegel, no matter how much the social order improves, it will never eliminate the alienation of the subject. This alienation is constitutive of subjectivity, which is why no society can do without it. Marx, in contrast, theorizes the arrival of a future society that solves the problem of alienation.

In his discussion of the differences between Hegel and Marx on the problem of alienation, Shlomo Avineri lays out the danger lurking within Marx's conception. In *Hegel's Theory of the Modern State*, he writes, "while Hegel sees alienation as a necessary aspect of objectification, Marx maintains that alienation does not reside immanently in the process of production itself, but only in its concrete historical conditions. For Marx, therefore, there exists the possibility of ultimate salvation, whereas for Hegel one will never be able to dissociate the cross from the rose of the present."[20] Although Hegel believes that we can better the conditions in society, he rejects the image of salvation implicit in Marx's vision of the communist future. If alienation is the condition of possibility for freedom, then there can be no future communist society free from alienation. The attempt to construct such a society would necessarily end in catastrophe.[21]

The difference between Hegel and Marx is the difference between a structural and a historical conception of alienation. If one conceives of alienation as structural and thus as constitutive for the subject, the response is to formulate a politics that doubles down on it rather than one which tries to eliminate it. We formulate a politics of alienation in response to the parade of purported cures for it.

Althusser vs. Lukács

Many followers of Karl Marx distance themselves from his analysis of capitalism as a system that imposes alienation on the working class. According to this line of Marxist thinking critical of the early Marx, the recourse to the concept of alienation seems to bespeak the early Marx's residual investment in a humanism that he inherited from Hegel and which he would later shed when he wrote *Capital*, his masterpiece. Foremost among these critics, Louis Althusser envisions an epistemological break occurring during Marx's intellectual trajectory. According to Althusser, one can distinguish between the young humanistic Marx — the Marx focused on alienation within capitalism — and the mature scientific one who analyzes the structure of capitalism without any critique of alienation. This turn supposedly marks a major advance in Marx's thinking and his critical capacity.

For Althusser, insisting on an epistemological break in the evolution of Marx's thought is not just an academic exercise. It is the key to constructing a Marxism that isn't humanistic, a Marxism that could transcend Marx's early moral critique of capitalism and rise to the level of science. In *For Marx*, an attempt to clearly delineate between the young and the mature Marx, Althusser attributes the concept of alienation to the influence of Feuerbach, not to Marx's own distinctive thinking about capitalism. He writes, "Marx's early works are impregnated with Feuerbach's thought. Not only is Marx's terminology from 1842 and 1845 Feuerbachian (alienation, species being, total being, 'inversion' of subject and predicate, etc.) but, what is probably more important, so is the basic *philosophical problematic*."[22] For Althusser, Marx remains within philosophy while talking about alienation and moves to scientific analysis when he gives this up as his thought matures and becomes his own.

Althusser shies away from the concept of alienation because it ties Marx to what he views as a naïve conception of the human. The early Marx who criticizes capitalist alienation is someone who accepts that there is something essential to humanity, a human essence, which the development of communism will recover. During this phase, Marx's theory of history envisions it moving toward the progressive overcoming of alienation. But Althusser sees this as clearly unsustainable on theoretical grounds.[23] Althusser rejects the idea of an essence of the human from which we might become alienated. To accept such an essence is to submit to the very capitalist thinking that Marxism should be opposing.

Althusser's antihumanist Marxism invests itself in Marxist science, a science based on the analyses put forward in the three volumes of *Capital* and in other late works. By abandoning the problem of alienation, however, Althusser eliminates any connection between a Marxist analysis of capitalism and the political activity of the proletariat. Political activity requires ideology and cannot receive its motivation from the truths of Marxist science. This position contrasts Althusser with Hegelian Marxist Georg Lukács, who doubles down on the early Marx's investment in the problem of alienation.

By developing a version of Marxism that aims at overcoming alienation, Lukács bridges the gap between theory and practice in a way that Althusser cannot. Lukács formulates the most philosophically developed Marxist theory of alienation by giving Marx's thought a Hegelian twist. But like Marx, Lukács conceives of alienation as a deficit that society must overcome. In *History and Class Consciousness*, he describes the problem of capitalist society in terms of alienation. He states, "man in capitalist society confronts a reality 'made' by himself (as a class) which appears to him to be a natural phenomenon alien to himself."[24] Through theoretical awareness of alienation — what Lukács theorizes as class consciousness — the proletariat can put itself in the position to overcome it. This is possible because the proletariat, unlike the capitalist class, is both the object and the subject of history. It is alienated by being turned into an object, but it can overcome this alienation when it acts as the subject of history by engaging in revolutionary practice.

The distinction between Althusser's antihumanist Marxism

and Lukács' humanist Marxism establishes one primary battleline of leftist politics in the twentieth century. But neither thinker, not even the more Hegelian Lukács, is able to recognize alienation as an emancipatory process. Marx's analysis of capitalism goes awry when it theorizes alienation as a problem, and this remains essentially the same even after Marx abandons the term. As a result, the apparently extreme difference between Althusser and Lukács ends up dissipating. Neither theorizes emancipation in terms of alienation.

Watching the Detective

Even when the mature Marx abandoned all discussion of alienation, he kept in place the conception of capitalism's relationship to labor that he used in his earlier analysis, in which this concept was central. In other words, although the mature Marx no longer talks about the alienation of human essence under capitalism, he remains within the structural logic of alienation: capitalism must be overcome, he argues, because it is a system that takes away from the working class what the working class itself produces. Marx's position here criticizes capitalism for being an alienating structure, even though he no longer employs the term *alienation* in his analysis.[25]

This is what Louis Althusser's idea of an epistemological rupture in Marx's trajectory overlooks. The break that Althusser introduces to distinguish a humanist Marx from a scientific Marx is not so much of a break at all. It is true that all references to alienation disappear after the *Economic and Philosophic Manuscripts of 1844*, which is why Althusser locates Marx's epistemological break in 1845, around the time of the writing of *The German Ideology*. And yet, the critique of capitalism that Marx develops in the *Grundrisse* of the 1850s and the three volumes of *Capital* has a formal homology with what Marx works out in the *1844 Manuscripts*. What he earlier calls the worker's alienation he comes to call the capitalist's appropriation of the surplus value that the worker produces. This is clearly a distinction, but it is not as dramatic a distinction as Althusser would have us believe.

Marx begins the first volume of *Capital* by unlocking the secret of the commodity. His development of the labor theory of value, taken from political economists Adam Smith and David Ricardo, leads to the concept of surplus value. Surplus value represents the key to Marx's contribution to the labor theory of value, which goes beyond what either Smith or Ricardo could conceive. The benefits of this concept are self-evident. It permits Marx to avoid just inveighing against capitalism on moral grounds. What's more, by analyzing the appropriation of the surplus value produced by labor, he can quantify capitalist exploitation. The capitalists exploit laborers to the extent that they appropriate the surplus value that the laborer produces without providing any remuneration for this creative act. The capitalists take what they don't pay for, which undermines the notion — fundamental to the justification of capitalism — of the free market. The market of equal exchange does not exist for the worker, who becomes impoverished through this exchange, or for the capitalist, who profits from the inequality. Marx's indictment of capitalism gains a firmer foothold thanks to the analysis of surplus labor time and the surplus value that it produces.

The concept of surplus value also gives Marx (and those following him) a concrete way to define ideology, even though he himself doesn't make use of it. Marx never uses the term *ideology* in *Capital* or in his later writings. But with the distinction that he makes between profit and surplus value, we can easily formulate a theory of ideology that inheres within the structure of capitalism. Capitalism functions ideologically insofar as it translates surplus value into profit, thereby enabling us to avoid seeing the role that labor plays in the creation of value.[26] Profit obfuscates labor. When capitalism as a system replaces surplus value with profit as the fundamental point of reference and the goal of everyone involved, it enables people to believe that profit is had through industriousness or through clever investing rather than through the accumulation of surplus value taken from workers.

That is to say, thinking in terms of profit rather than surplus value — the kind of thinking that capitalism requires — constitutes an alien form for thinking about how accumulation actually operates. Marx dedicates much of the third volume of *Capital* to an exploration of the relationship between surplus value and profit. There, he denounces profit as the disguised form of surplus value, a form that alienates workers from the value that their labor creates. He writes, "Profit, as we are originally faced with it, is thus the same thing as surplus-value, save in a mystified form, though one that necessarily arises from the capitalist mode of production."[27] By writing *Capital*, Marx hopes to counter the mystification that appears in the form of profit.

The alien form of profit disguises the fact that surplus value belongs to the worker who produces it rather than to the capitalist who appropriates it. Under capitalism, the problem is not just that we think in a mystified form about surplus value. It is that this value doesn't belong to the worker who creates it through excess labor. Capitalism is structured around the appropriation of the value created through work in excess of what it takes to sustain the society. This appropriation represents the alienation of surplus value from those who generate it.

Through the mechanism of capitalist production and exchange, surplus value undergoes a transformation into profit. Marx's effort in *Capital* is to trace profit back to its origins in surplus value and thus to the activity of the working class rather than the daring and ingenuity of the capitalist. Capitalism's focus on profit at the expense of surplus value allows this system to keep everyone invested in it despite the rampant inequality that it produces. In addition, the obfuscation of surplus value bespeaks the alienation of workers from the product of their labor. In the form of profit, their product appears in an alien form that disguises the real source of its value, which is the laboring act itself.

No matter how much the content of his critique changes, Marx's target is always the alien form that social relations take on within capitalist society. By shattering this alien form, he wagers, we can create a society in which we can develop the forces of production without any limit on their development. Capitalism moves toward but never reaches the universal development of society's productive capabilities. Communism, according to Marx, actually achieves this. In the *Grundrisse*, Marx envisions "a new mode of production," beyond capitalism, "where the free, unobstructed, progressive and universal development of the forces of production is itself the presupposition of society and hence of its reproduction; where advance beyond the point of departure is the only presupposition."[28] Production can become truly universal — that is, done for the sake of everyone — in the future society that the communist revolution will bring about. This vision of things is one in which human society would surpass the constraint of the alien force of capital pushing it in the direction of exploitation.

Even when Marx turns away from alienation in later works like the *Grundrisse*, he nonetheless holds fast to the way of thinking that animates his earliest critique of capitalist society. The problem with this society is that it artificially constrains our productivity with external limits that stem from its formal structure. By overthrowing it, we toss off the shackles of this alien power. Ending our capitalist alienation doesn't mean restoring a lost human essence but taking back the fruits of our own labor.

Hegel's Problems

Marx adopts a radically different approach to the emergence of problems than Hegel does. This difference stems from their distinct positions on alienation and has repercussions for how we conceive of political action. Marx sees the problems that crop up in human history and in thought as difficulties that have possible solutions. We can find these solutions if we analyze the problems scientifically rather than approaching them morally or technocratically.[29] After the proper scientific analysis, the solution requires revolutionary practice. We can solve the difficulties that we come up against in history because history presents us with solutions at the same time that it generates the problems. The trick is to interpret what's happening correctly and, importantly, not just content ourselves with a compelling interpretation.

In contrast to Marx, Hegel's sanguine view of alienation leads him to value the problem for its own sake. For Hegel, the proper attitude of the theorist to epistemological or historical problems is to treat the problem as its own solution. Rather than trying to eliminate the problem, Hegel discovers the solution to the problem within the problem itself. One must adopt a different position relative to the problem to accomplish this. Hegel doesn't think about the problem from the perspective of the solution but refuses to think outside the structure of the problem itself. The problem is its own solution when one looks at it dialectically. This produces a system that tries to change the world through the reinterpretation of the problems that it presents to us. Whereas Marx wants to change the world rather than merely interpret it, Hegel wagers that one changes it through the proper interpretation, an interpretation that frames the problem itself as the expression of a hidden contradiction.

Let's examine how this works in Immanuel Kant's distinction between appearances and things in themselves. In the *Critique of Pure Reason*, Kant insists that the subject can experience only appearances and can have no knowledge of things in themselves, except that they exist. This limitation on what it is possible for the subject to know has the paradoxical effect of freeing the subject from subjectivism. According to Kant, within the field of appearances, we can be certain about our objective knowledge, but this would be impossible if we took things in themselves as our objects. Skepticism about our ability to know things in themselves would destroy all possibility for objective knowledge.

Despite Kant's success in constructing a system that preserves objective knowledge from the skeptical critique (such as the one emanating from David Hume), he nonetheless runs into a stumbling block with the thing in itself.[30] Kant himself didn't recognize the difficulty, but later thinkers, from Fichte to Schelling to Hegel, were quick to do so. For Kant's system to work, the subject must be able to distinguish between appearances and things in themselves. But at the same time, the system requires the thing in itself to be completely unknowable for the subject. Kant thus grants the subject an ability to know that the thing in itself cannot be known, which it shouldn't be able to know if the thing in itself is really beyond the subject's arena of knowledge.

For Kant's most astute interpreters, the thing in itself is nothing but a representation of what cannot be thought, not an actual object. As Dieter Henrich points out, "what Kant means by the thing-in-itself is that there are no conditions affecting the essence of the givenness of things *per se*. The thing-in-itself is thus a limiting concept, because it designates what we cannot think."[31] Henrich recognizes that Kant isn't referring to an actual object when he posits the thing in itself, but even this generous interpretation runs into the problem of Kant conceptualizing what one cannot think. The act of formulating what lies beyond experience, even as a purely mental object, implies some ability to think beyond one's own thinking, which is impossible.

Hegel's response to the difficulty raised by the thing in itself is paradigmatic for his philosophy. He examines why this opposition between appearances and things in themselves emerges rather than trying to think through a way of escaping the opposition. This opposition comes about, he claims, because things always appear as if they are hiding an essence that is not readily apparent. Kant's conception of the thing in itself is the expression of the contradictions that create a disjunction within every appearance.[32]

Hegel doesn't seek a solution that would eliminate the problem. Instead, he discovers a line of thought that recognizes the solution inhering in the problem itself. Hegel's solution deepens the problem rather than lessening its impact. Ideology operates by telling us that problems can be surmounted, that difficulties can be avoided, as long as we adopt the proper policy. Hegel recognizes that while a problem might be surmounted, the problem of alienation cannot be. There is no exit from alienation to a situation in which the individual might be reconciled with the social order or in which the individual subject might be reconciled with itself. The key is to look at the problem differently — to see the problem as generative rather than just restrictive — which is what the theoretical intervention permits us to do. This requires recognizing that alienation is foundational.

At every point, Hegel's solution to historical and philosophical problems lies in taking the constitutive status of alienation as the unavoidable fact of subjectivity. Any solution that seeks to overcome alienation is always off the table. When he takes up this position, Hegel places himself at odds with those who would solve the problem of history. It's not enough, of course, to interpret problems from another angle to make them disappear. But this interpretive move frames how we conceive practical interventions. Political projects must insist on alienation as emancipatory and work through this conception.

For Marx, the situation is completely different. The task of the theorist is to point toward a solution to the problems that beset humanity because all our problems, including death, have a solution that will become apparent as history moves forward.[33] As a materialist, Marx does not believe that a mere theoretical act can solve the world's problems. There is no theoretical solution to our problems, but theory can suggest the avenue for material practice by highlighting the contradictions of the ruling socioeconomic system. This is what Marx attempts to do in his writings.

Marx insists that there is a solution, that our alienated

relations can be transformed through revolutionary practice. Human history has a solution thanks to the revolutionary possibility contained in the working class. In the *Economic and Philosophic Manuscripts of 1844*, Marx writes, "Communism is the riddle of history solved, and it knows itself to be this solution."[34] But Marx goes even further than this in his claims. Not only does communism solve the riddle of history, it also eliminates alienation from the natural world. According to Marx, "Communism… is the *genuine* resolution of the conflict between man and nature and between man and man."[35] Marx admits that individual conflicts between people will continue to exist within communist society, but he wagers that antagonistic conflict in the social order or between humanity and nature will disappear. The problems that seem fundamental to us today will find a solution in radical social change.

All our problems are soluble because our problems emerge out of the material conditions that also contain the solutions. As he puts it in the preface to the *Contribution to the Critique of Political Economy*, "Mankind thus inevitably sets itself only such tasks as it is able to solve, since closer examination will always show that the problem itself arises only when the material conditions for its solution are already present or at least in the course of formation."[36] Here, Marx envisions theoretical problems as tasks for political practice.[37] The theoretical problem arises in order to reveal the possibility of the practical act that would solve it. If we couldn't solve it, according to Marx, we would not even be able to register it as a problem. He thinks through problems from the perspective of their solutions, whereas Hegel thinks through solutions that never deviate from the problems themselves.

Marx's solution to the problem of the commodity does not follow Hegel's path. Instead, he identifies a secret force within the commodity that is the source of its creative power. Every commodity hides an act of theft, and Marx plays the detective who uncovers the theft and exposes the criminal. As Marx sees it, every commodity contains the unpaid surplus labor of the working class. This interpretation paves the way for the revolution that will rectify this crime and undo the injustices of commodity logic.

The Last Duel

The relationship between Hegel and Marx is not just an academic question. It concerns how we conceive of and embark on social change. If the ideal animating efforts at transforming society is putting an end to alienation or solving the riddle of human history, we are apt to see this goal as being worth whatever it might cost. For Hegel, on the contrary, the goal is inseparable from the means of arriving at it. In fact, the goal is nothing but the means we use to accomplish it. We are always arriving at our destination without ever getting there.

Another way of saying this is that Hegel is a dialectical thinker about emancipation, whereas Marx is more a dualistic one. Hegel envisions emancipation in alienation. Marx theorizes emancipation as the triumph over alienation. According to Marx, our alienated present is different in kind from the unalienated future. Or, the realm of freedom is fully distinct from the realm of necessity.

Marx's most conspicuous turn away from constitutive alienation occurs toward the end of the third volume of *Capital*. In a famous passage, Marx distinguishes between the realm of necessity and the realm of freedom. So far, so good. But as he describes these two realms, it becomes clear that he conceives them as absolutely distinct from each other. The realm of freedom doesn't emerge dialectically from the contradictions in the realm of necessity, nor does necessity reimpose itself as the contradictions in the realm of freedom become evident. Instead, Marx theorizes the relationship between these two realms dualistically: the realm of freedom starts where the realm of necessity ends, and there is no dialectical movement from one realm to the other.

Although Marx doesn't use the term when discussing the relationship between necessity and freedom, his conception of alienation lurks in the background of this analysis. Necessity necessarily implies alienation. As long as necessity compels me in a certain direction, I am alien to myself or under the control of an alien force. This is what Marx refuses to integrate into the realm of freedom, which is why he must separate it from the realm of necessity. Necessity cannot contaminate the realm of freedom with its alien power. If it does, then, in Marx's accounting, freedom wouldn't really be freedom.

For Marx, freedom becomes real freedom when it escapes the force of necessity. Or as he puts it in perhaps the most important passage from the third volume of *Capital*, "[there] always remains a realm of necessity. The true realm of freedom, the development of human powers as an end in itself, begins beyond it, though it can only flourish with this realm of necessity as its basis."[38] Marx correctly sees that humanity will not one day magically transcend the problem of necessity. He is not Ray Kurzweil.[39] But he does conceive the realm of freedom as a realm in which humanity rationally determines itself and its relationship to nature. Such a realm can have nothing to do with necessity because the presence of any necessity indicates an absence of freedom.

If we could have a realm of freedom distinct and separate from the realm of necessity, we should go to any lengths to bring this realm about. But if the realm of freedom always remains embroiled within the realm of necessity, how we bring it about matters just as much as its eventual emergence, since it will never fully emerge. Understood in this way, the realm of freedom is not a future to be achieved but a way of struggling within the realm of necessity. How we fight matters more than what we accomplish.

The embrace of alienation as emancipatory marks a turn from Marx back to Hegel. At the same time, it puts us in a position to think about emancipation not as a future to be achieved but as a different way of relating to the present. We can recognize not just that we don't fit within the present but that we cannot fit in any social order. The failure to fit is not a situation to be remedied but the condition of possibility for emancipation.

Chapter Five
From Community to
the Public

Out in the World

The embrace of alienation leads us to an existence as public beings. The alienated subject is displaced and outside of itself. As a result, this subject, when we recognize it, becomes open to the encounter with other alienated subjects, an experience that constitutes the public. Every time that an alienated subject encounters another, a public world emerges. Even if the public quickly closes down as the parties retreat back into their symbolic identities, its momentary emergence exhibits what equality and solidarity look like. They involve being together in a shared alienation. To pay attention to one's alienation is to engage in the recognition of the public in an era that incessantly denigrates it.

Jürgen Habermas was the first to theorize the public sphere as a political site where an egalitarian logic rules. Even though it violates this pledge by keeping many people out and giving more weight to the views of certain privileged voices, the public sphere promises universal access and equal weight to every idea articulated there. For Habermas, the ideal of the public sphere has an egalitarian social effect in spite of its failure to live up to the standard that it sets for itself. But he sees the public sphere as an arena that has largely disappeared with the development of capitalist society. Even though capitalism helps to birth the public sphere, it also brings about its death.

In *The Structural Transformation of the Public Sphere*, Habermas details the assault on the public sphere by the forces of capital. This happens primarily through the domination of the commodity form and its imprint on everything. Once the members of the public become purely consumers thinking in terms of the commodity, the public sphere effectively disappears. Or as Habermas puts it, "When the laws of the market governing the sphere of commodity exchange and of social labor also pervaded the sphere reserved for private people as a public, rational-critical debate had a tendency to be replaced by consumption, and the web of public communication unraveled into acts of individuated reception, however uniform in mode."[1] The logic of the commodity disperses the public sphere into isolated individualized acts that cease to bring people together in a world underwritten with egalitarian ideals. For Habermas, bourgeois culture generates the public sphere as a site for contestation and debate, and then capitalist society destroys it as the reach of commodification extends everywhere.

In the history of the bourgeois public sphere that Habermas relates, it develops primarily in privileged spaces, such as coffee houses and salons. When one enters these spaces, according to Habermas, one retains one's private identity while at the same time turning that private identity toward the public. Private people form a public by advancing their own opinions in a place where every opinion ideally has an equal weight.

Habermas's understanding of the public sphere, as important as it clearly is, undersells both the breadth of the public and the alienation required to produce it.[2] The public occurs through the encounter between alienated subjects who turn away from their private concerns to engage with others. When we are in the public, we are alienated from our private selves. This alienation is what constitutes a public no matter where it occurs. Through this shared alienation that distances us from our social positions, we discover the basis for universal equality. As public, alienated beings, no one has any more status than anyone else. The recognition of alienation connects us to everyone else.

The barrier to the recognition of alienation that constitutes the public is our investment in the idea of community. No one can avoid being part of a community, just as no one can avoid alienation. But the problem concerns where our investment lies. When we invest ourselves in a community and in the symbolic identity that a community provides, we fail to attend to the alienation that undermines all communal identity. The investment in community is an investment in having a social place. It is an investment that obfuscates our displacement and thereby hides the public. To believe that one belongs to a community is to fail to recognize the universality of alienation, a universality in which everyone is equal.

A community provides a larger context in which the subject is not simply alone with itself but has others to provide support for its identity. As a form, a community promises belonging, no matter what its size or what its specific content. It never delivers on this promise, however, which is why the public emerges. Community seems secure, and the public seems dangerous. But community and the public exist in a dialectical relation: the public exists through the community's failure to fully constitute itself. There is a public because there is no self-identical community. Further, there is community because no one can exist purely in a state of alienated subjectivity.

Once we take the constitutive alienation of subjectivity into account, we must look at community differently. Communities form around the effort to avoid the problem of alienation, the problem that inheres in subjectivity. Even though this effort always fails, the investment in the communal overcoming of alienation has deleterious consequences. It turns our focus away from our shared alienation and the equality that derives from it.

Communities promise respite from the burden of subjectivity by giving subjects a symbolic position with which to identify. Every symbolic identity depends on some community that authorizes and supports it. Without a community behind it, an identity would be meaningless. Identity exists through the recognition that the community gives it.

A community lays down a path leading from alienated subjectivity to symbolic identity. It offers its members the promise of belonging to encourage them down this path. The basic act of every community is to bestow a symbolic identity on the subjects that accede to its dictates and enter into it. When one identifies with the community and takes up a position within it, the problem of alienated subjectivity seems to dissipate. Alienation appears to be a difficulty that one might overcome through increasing identification with the community and one's symbolic position in it. Thanks to the community's intercession, I do not feel condemned to forever be an alienated subject but believe that I can have a valuable symbolic identity. The problem of who I am disappears beneath the position that I have. Subjectivity's question about who the subject is finds an answer in the identity that the community provides.

This contrasts community with the public. Unlike the community, the public foregrounds the alienation of the subject. It is a space — either physical or intellectual — that no one owns and that anyone can access, even though certain interests attempt to own it and to deny access to it.[3] The public is constantly under assault in capitalist society because it represents an egalitarian threat to capitalism's demand that we remain merely private beings.

It is because no particular group controls it that the public exists as the terrain where alienated subjectivity, not symbolic identity, becomes foregrounded. In the public, the subject cannot rely on its symbolic identity but must confront others without this support. When I'm in a public park, for instance, I might encounter someone I don't like or someone whose beliefs run counter to mine. But I have no power to exclude this person from the park. The public status of the park indicates that it is open to everyone, no matter what community a person belongs to. As a result, one finds oneself constantly in question. Through public engagement, the subject explores who it is through its engagement with others confronting the same problem.

Clearly, even a public park is not equally accessible to everyone. Those who live nearby or own a car to drive to it have more access. But the idea of the public park is that no one can be excluded because of their symbolic identity. No one is too poor to enter the park, nor is anyone too unseemly or unkempt. An idea of universal equality underlies the existence of this public space.[4]

It is important to cultivate the public because it provides a universality that no community even holds as an ideal. As a member of the public, my symbolic identity counts for nothing. I might be a Methodist or a member of the Elks, but this doesn't give me any priority to use the swing set in a public park or to check out books in a public library. Neither the swing set nor the books are mine. Everyone doesn't have them equally because we are all alienated from what exists in the public realm. I am alone with the singularity of my subjectivity, but it is precisely this singularity that connects me universally with everyone else. The absence of any necessary exclusion allows the public to evince a universality. Because the public offers us no way to belong, it doesn't have recourse to keeping some people out.

No one can have an alienation advantage over another, and alienation is the basis for participation in the public. The public provides a rampart against the community's inegalitarian distribution of identities. Every community survives by keeping certain people out, but the public is open to everyone. If not, it ceases to be truly public, which occurs when a neighborhood places a gate at the road leading into it or a lock on its swimming pool. The public's openness prevents it from offering assurances to the subject about what it is. As a member of the public, I am no one in particular but universally singular. Public interactions leave one uncertain about who one is because one encounters others who challenge one's identity. I might get into an argument on a public road, and my interlocutor could ask me, "Who do you think you are?" The logic of the public doesn't permit me to answer, "I'm a man, that's why I talked rudely to you." This recourse to my community — in this case, the community of men — violates the logic that governs the interaction. Of course, I can respond this way, but if I do so, I'm retreating from the public into my community. The community, in contrast to the public, seduces the subject by promising a clear answer to this and every question.

The structure of communities becomes clear if we look at them in relation to the subjects they accommodate. My national community tells me that there is no question about who I am because I'm an American. I can take solace in my Americanness no matter where I am in the world. My American passport offers me assurance in this regard, but even without it, I know myself to be an American. As a result, I always have a place where I belong, even when I'm detached from this place physically. For its part, the religious community obviates the question about my ultimate fate by telling me that I'm headed to heaven after death.[5] Instead of confronting death with anxiety, the trauma of the end becomes lightened through my community. My ethnic community, on the other hand, tells me where I come from and how to define myself in terms of my origins. Thanks to this framework, I do not have to regard myself just in terms of my uprooted subjectivity. A sexual community informs me that I'm heterosexual or homosexual and thus don't have to ponder the problem of where my desire lies. My community of friends reassures me that I am what I am, that my identity has an intrinsic validity.

In each case, the community provides protection from the unanswerable questions that subjectivity poses for itself. Subjectivity's nagging question receives a comforting answer in the form of a symbolic identity undergirded by the community. But one must look closely and see how every community ultimately fails to deliver the goods. The more I invest myself in a community, the more I sense that I don't belong. This alienation is what we must pay attention to.

"A Very Large Charge"

The community's protection from subjectivity comes with

a price. To receive the support that the community offers, I must submit to the implicit demands that hold it together. Members of any community, without exception, must obey its implicit demands. Most communities have explicit rules that they ask their members to abide by. Perhaps they even write these rules in a constitution or mount them in a prominent place to stress their importance. But it is the implicit demands that play the crucial role in community building. Sometimes the implicit demands tell members how to relate to the explicit rules — which ones to obey completely, which ones to disregard, and so on. Members don't make these demands public but keep them secret from outsiders. They don't even discuss them openly among themselves. The community's implicit demands create a bond through a shared secret that divides those in on it from those on the outside.[6]

We can look at a telling example: the secret, implicit demand that constituted the community formed around my college football team. A college football team is an exclusive community. Only those proficient enough at the sport can participate on a team at this level.[7] But this positive characteristic is not sufficient to constitute the communal bond. Something more is required — a secret demand that everyone must heed in order to belong.

On this football team (and many others, I assume), the implicit demand involved submission to a variety of homoerotic rituals in the locker room. These included players rubbing their penises against the naked bodies of other players, simulating anal sex with each other, engaging in performances showcasing their genital flexibility to everyone in the locker room, and grabbing the genitalia of their teammates, among other related acts. To be a member of the community formed around the team, one had both to participate in these activities and guard the secret of their existence. To broadcast the existence of these rituals would have entailed immediate expulsion from the community. Even to bring up their existence in a discussion with teammates would have threatened one's place in the community.

But it was not enough to refrain from speaking about the hidden homoeroticism. Keeping the secret also required a public face of rabid homophobia (or at least the quiet acceptance of the rabid homophobia of the other members of the community). Members of the football community acceded to the homoerotic rituals while at the same time publicly rehearsing hostility to any homosexual activity. There was a direct contradiction between the public attitude of the players toward homosexuality and their adherence to the implicit demand that required an embrace of homosexual activity. But no one outside the community could know about this contradiction. This is how the implicit demand divided those who belonged from those on the outside. The shared secret of the ritual enjoined by the community's implicit demand played an essential role in constituting the community.

Even though the coaches did not participate in any of the homoerotic rituals or have direct knowledge of them, they did their part to keep up the homophobic face of the team. On the bus traveling to a game one week, I wore a shirt celebrating "Pink Triangle Week," a campus event supporting the gay and lesbian struggle. Before the bus started, one otherwise mild-mannered coach walked back to me and said, "Get that fucking shirt off right now." This coach's statement indicated the extent to which the shirt violated the community's implicit demand. The slightest chink in the armor of the united front of homophobia represented a mortal danger to the community and had to be dealt with severely.

The coach's reprobation made it clear to me that while wearing that shirt I was not fully part of the community, that I didn't belong. And yet, despite this moment of ostracism, I did not leave the community. I did not completely abandon my symbolic identity as a member of the team. My marginal position relative to the other players left me caught between embracing alienation and striving to belong. This is the existential bind that confronts everyone: no one can abandon community and identity altogether, but everyone has the potential to recognize the priority of alienation relative to the attempt to belong.

While not every community operates with an implicit demand as contrary to its public face as this college football team in the late 1980s, no community can do without a secret implicit demand that creates exclusivity. Communities must be exclusive, and only secret implicit demands can create exclusivity. In the case of nations or ethnic communities, this is often the shared disdain for the national or ethnic outsider. But even the most open community makes an implicit demand on its members that none can forgo while remaining members. The community provides the security of a symbolic identity while forcing the subject to pay for this security with strict obedience. No community offers identity for free.

Obedience entails opposing the outsiders who play a constitutive role for the community through their position as outsiders. In the case of the college football team, the outsiders were not, as one might suppose, the opposing teams. The players on other teams belonged to the college football community and, we should figure, participated in the same homoerotic rituals. The outsiders were those who challenged the heterosexual masculinity that constituted the community surrounding the team.[8] By dint of the outsiders, the community gains its exclusivity. Some belong, while others remain outside. Without those on the outside, belonging would lose its luster. Community membership has a value insofar as it is particular and exclusive. It requires a barrier between inside and outside.

This is especially true in communities that never recognize themselves as communities. Think, for instance, of the white community. Most members of the white community don't think of themselves as part of a community at all.[9] This community does not form around the skin color of its members but through the actions that indicate an obedience to the implicit demands that it makes on them. Making racist statements, listening to racist conversations without objection, and participating in racist actions all constitute the white community. Whiteness alone does not suffice.[10] The white community has no public rules guiding behavior because it denies its status as a community. But the existence of implicit demands surrounding whiteness reveals that it is a community all the same.[11] Like every community, it is exclusive. Its implicit demands are there to enforce this exclusivity. One must prove that one psychically aligns oneself with the community by obeying the demands that define it. There is no belonging without obedience. One turns to the community for the freedom to be oneself, and one finds a demand for capitulation.

The additional problem, however, is that the security the community provides is always illusory. No symbolic identity can ever relieve one of the problem of alienated subjectivity. Even within the comforts of a community and the identity that it offers, one remains an alienated subject. The problem persists. The community gives me a symbolic identity, but that identity ends up being at odds with itself. Its security is ultimately insecure.

In this sense, community is fool's gold. We invest ourselves in community to escape the problem of alienation, but this problem returns with a vengeance when we experience our failure to belong to the community. It always appears to us as if others really belong while we are stuck in the position of striving to belong. Community doesn't succeed because no one can ever become secure in their belonging. Alienation always trumps identity. The problem with an investment in community is that it encourages us to turn away from the pinch of alienation rather than recognize ourselves in this discomfort.

Let's return to the community of the college football team. The players on the team gain a symbolic status by virtue of their membership in the community. They strive to belong, while others who they encounter are outside their community of belonging. Their symbolic position seems completely secure. They have masculinity, violence, and a close-knit community all on their side. But the identity is completely tenuous. At any point, the secret of the homoerotic rituals could become public, or a particular player might reveal himself as insufficiently masculine to belong. What's worse, no one ever experiences himself as an authentic member of the community. No one is ever cool enough. In this community — as in every community — one's belonging is always on trial.

Far from providing the security that it promises, symbolic identity puts one at constant risk. The subject occupying an identity never knows if it is doing enough to sustain its position. In order to save their own symbolic position, the members of the community might resort to excluding me. This might happen at any time, such as when I wore the unwelcome shirt on the football team's bus. The precariousness of symbolic identity leaves me always on the brink of losing it. Symbolic identity offers an image of security that it never delivers. But we keep returning to it on the basis of the image that it holds out to us.

The public realm makes no promises of security.[12] The insecurity of alienation is apparent in every public interaction. When I have a conversation in a public park, I do so without the security of my private domain or the assurance that the person with whom I'm talking belongs to my community. They could find my jokes offensive, mock my Midwestern accent, or simply turn away from me altogether. My symbolic identity loses its protective power in the public.

But the public enables us to discover a bond with others that doesn't rely on our rickety, symbolic identities. It forges a connection through alienation, not through its obfuscation. The fact that no one is at home in the public makes it a site where equality can become evident. The public enables me to escape the hierarchies that control communities and interact as a free subject. I am able to act freely in the public because the constraints of my community do not hold sway there. Everyone can share equally in this freedom as long as no community prevails over the public realm. In the public, we are alone together, which is the only possible form of solidarity.[13]

Meet the New Boss

A community or culture forms through the assertion of a master signifier that holds the community together. The community requires this signifier because it gives the community a point through which it can identify itself. This foundational term — like *American*, *Haitian*, *Korean*, or, say, college football player — provides an organizing site for the community that gives it a symbolic starting point. Everyone can point to this one signifier as the foundation for an identity within the community. This master signifier has no signification itself, no signified. One cannot say what it means to be American, Haitian, or Korean, for example. The signifier acquires a signification only through establishing a position of nonbelonging, encompassing those who it excludes from its field. A particular community's identity is constituted through what it is not. I know that I am an American because I know that I'm not a communist. I know that I am a German because I know that I'm not a Jew. Or even: I know that I am a Korean because I know that I'm not Japanese. This act of creating a position of nonbelonging is the prerequisite for all identity within a community. I belong through those who don't. There is no community identity that does not refer to figures of nonbelonging to secure the identity of those who belong.

Champions of particular identity must vehemently denounce the outsider that threatens the community or culture that they want to uphold. The figure of nonbelonging does represent a threat, but this threat is necessary for the community or culture to constitute itself. There is no particular community that can survive without a figure of nonbelonging that threatens that particular identity.

The reliance of community on the threat that would destroy it is evident in the case of right-wing extremist movements. Nativist movements typically use the signifier of the nation's name as a rallying point. This name serves as a master signifier for such movements. But at the same time, this master signifier would remain meaningless for them without another signifier that identifies those who don't belong to the community. The immigrants who threaten the security of the national community in the eyes of the nativist are actually the sine qua non of that community. They threaten it into existence. The master signifier alone is not enough.

This is why Donald Trump began his 2016 presidential campaign with the promise to build a wall to keep immigrants from the south out of the United States. Trump proclaimed that he would "Make America Great Again," but the vehicle for doing this was establishing a negative relation to immigrants. Without the immigrant to determine what America signifies, Trump's appeal for renewed American greatness would have fallen on deaf ears. The master signifier can only structure a community when it has a figure to define itself against.

Despite the political opposition between liberalism and nativist movements, the same dynamic holds true for liberalism. The liberal community can only exist as a community insofar as some entity threatens it. This position aims at total inclusion, the construction of a community so large that it will have no one left outside. But the ideal of bringing everyone inside — achieving total inclusivity — is a liberal fantasy that requires someone to play the heavy and continue to threaten the liberal community. Liberal openness cannot exist without walls, no more than the America made great again that Donald Trump envisions.

When Hillary Clinton denounced the "basket of deplorables" during the 2016 presidential campaign, she inadvertently hit on a structural necessity implicit in the liberal position that she embodied. Clinton spoke a truth that needed to remain unsaid because it articulates the impossibility of the inclusivity that the liberal champions.[14] The liberal community depends on the deplorables threatening it because these figures of liberal nonbelonging give significance to liberal identity, which would otherwise be bland and meaningless. It would otherwise not be an identity at all. There are always deplorables somewhere giving liberalism an outsider to define itself against, but they typically remain unnamed.

Inclusivity works only insofar as it remains a total inclusivity to come. The moment that we realized this ideal, it would collapse as a tenable position because there would be no one to occupy the necessary point of nonbelonging that holds the group together. Even for those who belong to a community that values inclusivity, the community can only provide identity through the position that doesn't belong to it. Without this position, belonging ceases to have a meaning.

All community depends on at least one particular being excluded. In this sense, every community is a gated community, no matter how open and welcoming it appears. Rather than being an oxymoron as some critics label it — "If it's gated, it's not really a community" — the gated community has a paradigmatic status relative to all other communities.[15] Communities form through keeping people out. If they fail to do this, if they are open to everyone, they cease to be communities and become public. It is impossible to conceive of a community that avoids the act of exclusion.

This is illustrated by a joke about communism that reveals how even the proponents of communism — a project that aims at overcoming all exclusion — can operate in terms of the particular community. In this joke, Marx approaches Lenin in heaven to discuss Lenin's attempt to realize a Marxist vision of things in Russia. Marx congratulates him and says, "You seized power for communism just as I imagined. You introduced economic changes at just the right pace. You even worked to transform the political thinking in the country. Great job. But now the revolution really seems to be Stalin." While this joke clearly signals an allegiance to the universal communist project, it succumbs to the logic of the community in the way that it positions Stalin in relation to the communist project. Every community — the communist community in this joke — depends on the outsider to act as the focal point for the community's identity.

Here, communism appears as a project that might come off without contradiction were it not for Stalin gumming up the proceedings. The joke never recognizes anything in the communist project itself that creates the space for the damage Stalin did to it, which is why we should see this as ultimately a particularist joke, a joke that conceives of communism as the work of a community. Stalin is the problem to be overcome, but there is no articulation of how the interruption is the point where the public forms. Despite Marx being an avowed universalist, his attempt in the joke to put the blame on Stalin for communism's failure marks a turn toward the particularism of the community. That said, it hardly seems fair to blame Marx for what he says in a joke that I made up. But this is a position that many Marxists take up relative to Stalin. In this sense, the joke reveals how communal thinking trumps a universalist interpretation of events even among professed universalists.

Communities offer members recognition in exchange for their identification with the symbolic positions that the community makes available to them. But the community forms not through those it admits but through those it doesn't. There can be no universal community, no community without outsiders. Those who don't belong provide the cement that holds every community together. The public, in contrast to the community, is much more fragile because it lacks the outsiders that the community has.

Get on the Bus

The contrast between the public and the community manifests itself most clearly in the distinction between the public bus and the chartered one. When I ride a public bus, I encounter people I don't know. I might be sitting next to a talkative stranger when I want to sleep. I must adjust my own schedule to that of the bus. I don't have any privileges relative to the other riders, no matter what my symbolic status outside the bus. Anyone can ride — rich or poor, Chinese or Brazilian, intelligent or not so much, clean or dirty, Muslim or Buddhist, and so on ad infinitum. Anyone can ride because no particular community or person owns the mode of transportation. The public bus is a site of alienation, which is why many people refuse to ride.[16]

Unlike the private airline, the public bus does not seat people according to their symbolic status. One cannot buy a first class ticket on the public bus but must sit wherever there is an open space. The open seating policy can result in one finding oneself seated next to someone from a completely different community. A Catholic anti-Semite might find herself seated next to a Jew. An Israeli resident of the West Bank colonies might find himself seated next to a Palestinian. A Palestinian Muslim might find herself seated next to a vehement atheist. And on and on. The public status of the bus implies that there is always a possibility that one could confront what one doesn't wish to confront. The public bus is an alien terrain for everyone riding.

One of the keys to the public realm manifests itself on the public bus. This is the lack of an assigned place for anyone. The fact that I must sit in an open seat — or not sit at all if the bus is crowded — indicates that there is no place for me on the bus. The public is an alienated space for everyone, a space in which everyone is displaced. A public bus has seats but not places, nowhere for the subject to feel at home. The absence of place permits the public to be a site of freedom.

In the public space of the bus, the alienated subject comes to the fore. At the same time, one's symbolic identity forged through the community counts for nothing. There is an inherent vulnerability that one experiences on the bus because one rides without the security of this symbolic identity. One cannot be at home on the public bus, even though public laws — prohibiting assault, hate speech, sexual violence, and theft, among other things — govern this space.

We can see the effect of the public status of the bus in the ways that people attempt to retreat from it. One person puts on headphones to listen to music, while another goes to sleep. Someone stares at their phone, and someone else looks out the window to avoid engaging anyone else inside. These gestures are efforts to escape the encounter with the public and the alienation that it entails. But the most egregious form of recoil from the public on the bus is the official decision to allow community to obtrude on this space.

There are times when the community imposes itself wholly on the public bus. This occurred in the Jim Crow South of the United States. The public bus in the South distributed its seats according to the community of the riders. Those belonging to the white community could ride in the front, while those belonging to the Black community had to ride in the back of the bus. Even though the bus was public in name, the symbolic status of the white community eviscerated its public status.

The Civil Rights movement was an effort to strip away the white community's dominance of the public. It foresaw a genuine public wherein one community could not assert itself over another. Rosa Parks was a leader in the struggle to make the public bus public. She stands as an icon of the Civil Rights movement for her refusal to give up her seat to a white person on a public bus in Montgomery, Alabama.[17] Through her act of defiance, Parks insisted that the authorities in Montgomery recognize the public status of the bus, that they cease allowing the white community to dominate this public space.

While the segregated bus reflects the community's undermining of the public, the chartered bus represents a site where the community rules without any contact with the public. Community dominates the chartered bus even more than it does the segregated one. The chartered bus contrasts dramatically with the public bus. Let's look at the chartered bus for the college football team, which we used to travel to games played away from our home stadium. This bus allowed members of the football community to be at home with themselves. Sometimes the trips were quite long — up to twelve hours — but one always had a place during this time. Players could be sure to sit where they wanted to sit, associate with those they wanted to associate with, and take part in all the activities of the community, albeit in a confined space.

Unlike the public bus, the chartered bus protects the community from the alienation of the public. On the team's chartered bus, there was no risk that one's homophobic slurs might arouse public disapprobation. Rather than sitting alone in one's seat, one could shoot craps clandestinely in the back of the bus. The community could engage in crude ritual chants that singled out certain players or the upcoming opponent. Most importantly, one experienced the other riders on the bus as part of one's community, which granted one an ability to act impulsively in the ways that the community endorsed or permitted.

The chartered bus obscures alienation, while the public bus highlights it. When we consider the relationship between these two related forms of travel, the contrast between the public and the community becomes clearer. Even though the public bus leaves the rider displaced, it reveals the rider's alienated subjectivity through this displacement. On the chartered bus, riders can have a place. But to have a place, they must obey the dictates of the community and acquiesce to its complete inequality. Chartering turns the potentially public bus into a land version of the cruise ship.

One of the most important questions in the history of cinema is why *Speed* (Jan de Bont, 1994) is so superior to its sequel, *Speed 2: Cruise Control* (Jan de Bont, 1997). The same director created both films, and each stars Sandra Bullock. Jason Patric replacing Keanu Reeves as the male lead surely cannot account for the horrible falling off that occurs in the second film. If one considers the difference between the public bus that serves as the setting for the original film and the private cruise ship where the sequel takes place, the answer becomes clear. The public bus in *Speed* enables a universal connection to form among the riders in the film and the spectators watching it, whereas on the private cruise ship, it's each community for itself with the spectators left on the outside. One watches *Speed 2* with little concern for those on the ship because they remain ensconced within their private communities. In the original, those riding the bus constitute part of the alienated public, which facilitates the bond with everyone else, including spectators. They experience a level of discomfort with each other, but it is precisely this universal alienation that invites the spectator to be on the bus as well.

The cruise ship, like the chartered bus, attempts to create a secure communal space, which is why it cannot be open to those on the outside. The spectators of *Speed 2* are stuck on the outside, unlike those fortunate enough to ride along on the bus in *Speed*. The cruise ship suffers the fate of the chartered bus, only it amps up the problem by surrounding people with countless commodities to help ensconce them in their privacy.

The displacement that one endures on the public bus exposes a freedom and equality that the chartered bus works to hide. It feels better to ride a chartered bus: there is less worry about undesirable interlocutors or unwanted encounters. But the price of the chartered bus far exceeds what it costs to ride. When opting for a chartered bus rather than a public one, we choose the inequality of the community over the shared freedom of our alienation.[18]

Interrupted Togetherness

Most commonly, people link solidarity to a common human essence rather than to a shared alienation. This makes intuitive sense because alienation appears negative and the idea of a human essence initially seems positive. The defenders of this position range from humanists who attribute the human essence to humanity's position in the natural world to theists who identify it with the spark of divine creation. No matter what its philosophical origins, the notion of a common human essence has the virtue of attempting to include everyone within its conception of the human.[19]

This position was especially prominent at the beginning of modernity, from the seventeenth through to the end of the eighteenth century. In 1689, John Locke wrote his *Two Treatises on Government*, where he articulated a naturalist basis for a human essence. Freedom derives not from any particular characteristic that one might have but belongs to all as a result of their natural status as human. In the *Second Treatise*, Locke writes, "The *Natural Liberty* of Man is to be free from any Superior Power on Earth, and not to be under the Will or Legislative Authority of Man, but to have only the Law of Nature for his Rule."[20] According to this position, no one can enslave or subjugate another because to do so would violate the other's essential humanity that derives from nature itself.

One can arrive at this same position with recourse to God. The Declaration of Independence, founding the United States in 1776, attributes universal human values to the actions of a divine creator. Human rights are unalienable, according to this document, because people have been "endowed by their Creator" with them. According to this view, our human essence derives from the act of a transcendent being, which gives the rights that accompany it a secure basis.

The problem with locating the source of values in a shared human essence quickly becomes apparent if we examine the relationships of its authors. Locke invested in a slaveholding company and played a part in writing the constitution of a colony where slavery was legal. For his part, Thomas Jefferson, the primary author of the Declaration of Independence, owned slaves and governed a nation formed through the labor of slaves. The human essence didn't stop either Locke or Jefferson from excluding some from their conception of the human.

These are not just the isolated missteps of two theorists who failed in practice to live up to the values they held in theory. Whether one assumes that the human essence derives from God, from nature or from some other source, it cannot rise to the status of a universal. The image of a shared humanity with a single essence always necessitates an inhuman other that makes it possible to delimit the human. One defines what is essentially human through the contrast with the inhuman other. Any recourse to a shared human essence has to leave someone out of that essence.[21]

Alienation doesn't suffer from this defect. Our alienation is not the badge of belonging that excludes others but the indication of a failure that *eo ipso* cannot exclude anyone. The great virtue of failure is that everyone can do it, whereas inclusion requires a corresponding exclusion. Everyone partakes equally in the failure of alienation, no matter what their social or material status. The wealthiest experience alienation just as thoroughly as the most destitute. This is why the only bond that creates the possibility of universal solidarity is a bond of alienation. Alienation, the distance that separates people from each other and from themselves, is what they have in common. Alienation is universal. One's very ability to relate to oneself as a subject depends on the structure of alienation that inserts a distance in the heart of subjectivity.

The universality of alienation contrasts with the specificity of every community or cultural identity. Every cultural identity is particular and requires other cultural identities opposed to it that affirm its particularity. Martin knows that he is German insofar as he knows that Simone is French. The same logic applies to every form of cultural identity, even if the culture is one that can theoretically welcome all, such as goth culture or drug culture. Even the most open culture remains ensconced in its own particularity that must have other particular cultures opposed to it. Goth culture requires an opposing jock culture, and drug culture would not exist without a straight culture that it defines itself against.

But the particularity of our community does not imply that we are identical with this particularity. No one is identical with the community in which they exist. The universality of alienation interrupts every community and every cultural identity. The subject is always a stranger within its own community. A community is not a home that we comfortably inhabit but an alien shell that tries to convince us that we belong to it. Every community tries to pass for what it isn't.

Every community must resort to ritual and indoctrination in an effort to bridge the gap that separates them from the subjects that make them up. If we were simply identical with our culture, no inculcation would be necessary to ensure my belonging. I would not require confirmation to attest to my Catholicism, a bat mitzvah to mark my passage into Jewish adulthood, or hazing to affirm that I am part of the fraternity. The ritual designed to testify to belonging always does the opposite: it exposes the alienation of subjectivity from its community identity.

The public is what exposes every community as contradictory and self-undermining. What we all have in common is our inability to be identical with ourselves or with our community. Or one could say: What we have in common is what we don't have. Every community, every culture, is fundamentally at odds with itself. This contradiction is what provides the opening that enables one culture to speak to another. It is also the site of universality in the community. The community's contradiction is itself universal, but we miss it when we think of universality as something that we all have in common or something that contains all particular communities or cultures within it. The universal is not something that we can have or impose on others but a failure that inhabits every culture. The public inhabits this failure.

But when the vast majority of people retreat into their private communities, the public is at risk of dying out. It survives on the basis of people embracing their alienation enough to venture into the public and engage with other alienated subjects. To keep the public viable, subjects must be open to accepting their fundamental uprootedness. No matter how limited the public arena might be, it exists as long as alienation does. But the challenge is to recognize ourselves as public beings, an act that requires an embrace of alienation.

Without the public as a viable alternative to community, it becomes almost impossible to turn one's back on one's community. In this situation, it seems as if everyone is ensconced in their own private communities. One is a private entity surrounded by other private entities. There appears to be no other possibility.

The search for an identity that fully corresponds to who we are is an attempt to cure alienation. This is why all identitarian projects exhibit a horror of the public. The public gives the lie to all identity and undermines its pretentions to completion. Identity obscures the alienation of subjectivity by making the subject appear to be its identity. While the subject is out of joint with itself, identity creates the appearance of self-coincidence, even if an identity is one of permanent flux. By recognizing every identity as a failure, we can remain within the question of subjectivity itself, which is the public terrain.

To do so is to embrace the constitutive alienation of subjectivity, to embrace being out of place as one's only possible relationship to one's particular community. This requires becoming comfortable with being uncomfortable.

Only by accomplishing this can we sustain the universal problem of subjectivity without rushing toward a solution that will always make matters worse. Laying out how to act as a public being is Jane Austen's great achievement, as most of the films adapting her novels make clear.

Publicizing Jane Austen

We tend to think of Jane Austen as either a moralist or a novelist of romance. According to Juliet McMaster and numerous other critics of Austen, the salient feature of her narrative universe is moral order. McMaster says, "Jane Austen's world is morally ordered and fully significant, in ways that make us wistfully envious, as we muddle along with our messy lives in our permissive culture."[22] Those who look at Austen as a writer of romance fiction see her as offering new ways of thinking about love. For Austen, what's crucial is not the end point that the couple attains when they marry but the path that they traverse on the way. Thus, the narrative of her final novel, *Persuasion*, bases love on an initial failure, a failure integral to the relationship. Robyn Warhol describes Austen's *Persuasion* as "a story of lost love regained, of oppositions reconciled."[23] Austen uses the novel form to rethink morality and love, both of which are impossible for anyone who remains ensconced in privacy.

Both Austen's moralism and her depictions of romantic love occur in the public world. In Austen's fiction, morality and love are only possible when one accedes to the alienation that one undergoes in public. One never finds them within the closed space of one's own community. The universe of Jane Austen contains a public world which demands certain public virtues, but this public world also makes evident the emergence of alienated subjectivity. It is in the public, Austen shows, that the alienated subject reveals itself. Austen's celebration of this subject is simultaneously a defense of the public realm in which this alienated subject manifests itself.

Austen's heroes — Elinor Dashwood in *Sense and Sensibility*, Elizabeth Bennet in *Pride and Prejudice*, Anne Elliot in *Persuasion* — evince a deference to the public. Although it inflicts suffering on them because it exposes them to others who are hostile to them, they respect the public realm by enduring the alienation that it requires. Each of these women suffers because they cannot directly expose who they are to the world. What's more, they experience an internal barrier that prevents them from knowing themselves. While she remains ensconced in her own community, Elizabeth Bennet believes that she knows what she wants. It is only through the encounter with the public — and what she perceives as the rudeness of Mr Darcy — that she discovers her unconscious desire. Austen's heroes are alienated subjects who see themselves in their alienation rather than in the attempt to overcome it. They accept that they are public beings.

The characters Austen derides, in contrast, cling to their private identities that derive from community. They spend their time trying to shore up their symbolic position in the face of the alienating structure of the public. But the refusal to abandon their private selves leaves these characters — Mr Collins in *Pride and Prejudice* and Walter Elliot in *Persuasion*, to name just two of many — completely vapid. They are what their community tells them they are, and they cling to this symbolic identity even when in public. Austen shows that what makes a person compelling is precisely the ability to abandon symbolic identity for the sake of the alienating public world. Her novels provide a theoretical definition of inanity, something that no one prior to her could do. For Austen, an inane person is someone who clings to a symbolic identity instead of embracing the alienation of subjectivity.

There is a third category of characters in Austen's novels — the villains. These are the characters who use the alienation of the public realm to their own private advantage. Unlike the inane characters, the villains grasp that the public exists, but they try to put it to work for themselves. The opacity of relations in the public enables the villains, such as George Wickham in *Pride and Prejudice* and William Elliot in *Persuasion*, to manipulate others into their untoward schemes. George Wickham cons Lydia Bennet into running away with him even though he has no intention of marrying her. The disgrace that he brings on her violates the tenets of the public realm, but Wickham's only concern is the sexual conquest that will feed his symbolic identity. He never takes the risk of existing as an alienated subject in the public. Both the vapid characters and the villains fail to see that the alienation that takes place in the public doesn't take the subject away from its authentic self but reveals subjectivity. As the public strips away the value of symbolic identity, it frees the subject to break from the constraints of community. Seeking refuge in one's community and the identity it offers leaves one unable to recognize that there is nothing more authentic than alienation.

Austen's heroes recognize that one cannot act straightforwardly in the public. The alienation of the public realm necessitates indirection on the part of the subject, who must speak its desire in a way that circumnavigates the restrictions that the public world imposes. The public places a barrier between the subject and the object of its desire, but it is this barrier that enables the subject to recognize its love for that object. As Austen's novels reveal, the only love is an alienated love.[24]

The focus on the public in Austen's novels stands out in the film and television versions of them that have come out in the last thirty years. Most of the films and television series emphasize the political significance of the public realm as much or more than Austen herself does. Roger Michell's 1995 film version of *Persuasion* represents the high-water mark of this effort to show the importance of the public by adapting an Austen novel.[25] *Persuasion*, Austen's posthumously published final novel, depicts the relationship between Captain Wentworth and Anne Elliot, which they renew years after Anne rejected Wentworth on the advice of her trusted friend Lady Russell. Their relationship develops amid the insults and abuse that Anne must endure from her own family. She is an outsider even, or especially, at home. Anne's private community is completely oppressive, and the only respite that she has comes when she goes out in public. Even though Wentworth and Anne love each other from the start of the novel to the end, there are multiple obstacles blocking the consummation of this love, most notably the public world and the alienation that it manifests. The obstacles don't prevent their marriage, which concludes the novel. Despite the conventional ending, Austen shows that this marriage is a bond of equals because both partners embrace alienated subjectivity in their relations. Neither Anne nor Wentworth takes refuge in a symbolic identity, although they each, of course, have one. As a result, they often find themselves unable to say what they really feel to each other. The events of the entire novel take place against the background of this inability.

Revealing everything would suffocate the public world and make it uninhabitable. If one revealed all in public, the public world would disintegrate and become nothing but an amalgam of competing communal interests. When in public in the Austen universe, one must disguise oneself. Alienation is the primary requirement for a public existence. As a result, desire can exist only indirectly and within the gaps of the public world.

In the film version of *Persuasion*, we see how the public world puts up the barrier of conventions to the direct communication of desire. Anne Elliot (Amanda Root) cannot just tell Captain Wentworth (Ciarán Hines) how she feels, nor can he tell her directly. The public creates all sorts of miscommunications and mistakes in making one's desire known. Far from impairing the film, however, Anne and Wentworth's inability to articulate their desire is what generates the spectator's enjoyment.

Anne's father, Sir Walter (Corin Redgrave), and her sister, Elizabeth (Phoebe Nicholls), refuse to heed the requirements of the public realm. They cling to their communal identity and use public interactions to advance their private interests. On almost every occasion in which we see Sir Walter engaged in conversation, he is pontificating about the ugliness of the people he has seen. At the beginning of the film, he initially refuses to lease his estate to a sailor because he is offended by the toughened skin and hard looks of sailors.

Walter and Elizabeth openly articulate their private hostility toward Anne, despite the public prohibition on such displays. And yet, Anne does not reject the public or refuse to exist within it. Her response to her situation is public silence. Throughout the film, Anne continues to appear in public and to obey the rules of public conduct, never directly articulating her desire for Captain Wentworth. In fact, despite the complete isolation within which she lives, Anne is never alone in the film. We see her isolation in the visual field always against the background of a public. Her public silence neither offends her interlocutors nor engages them. Anne even maintains this public silence when others confront her with speculation about whom Captain Wentworth shall marry. The attitude of public silence — an attitude which obeys the public codes of conduct without any investment in them — shows Anne's acceptance of her public alienation, a position that the form of the film champions.[26]

One would think that the strict limitations that govern the public realm would make it a site of oppression for Anne. But the film reveals that her community — more specifically, her family — is much more oppressive than the public. Anne finds freedom in the alienating public that she doesn't have in her community. Her relationship with Wentworth occurs almost entirely in public. Even when we see the married couple together at the end of the film, she is by his side on a ship, not ensconced in a domestic situation where she would have a designated place.

The public world constantly puts up a barrier to the direct expression of one's desire. Despite her numerous meetings with Captain Wentworth throughout the film, neither he nor Anne can express their desire. This barrier exists between them even when they are engaged in a seemingly private conversation. Alone with Anne in a carriage, Captain Wentworth makes an abortive attempt at direct communication: "I regret that… damned foolish, damned foolish." Later, at a concert in Bath, Captain Wentworth again tries to tell Anne his desires — "Anne, I have never…" — only to be interrupted by the arrival of Lady Dalrymple (Darlene Johnson). When Captain Wentworth observes what he assumes to be intimacy between Anne and Mr Elliot (Samuel West) during the concert, he proceeds to head angrily toward the exit.

This type of misrecognition is a constant danger for Anne due to her alienated status. As Wentworth is leaving the concert, Anne tries to stop him, but she cannot say the one thing that would make him stay — that she loves him. This conversation is perhaps the most frustrating of the entire film because the spectator can only watch the failure to communicate while all along knowing the truth of Anne's desire. As it concludes, Anne pleads with Wentworth to stay, saying to him, "The next song is very beautiful. It's a very beautiful love song. Is that not worth your staying for?" Wentworth's reply — "There's nothing worth my staying for" — makes evident the failure of Anne's efforts. She fails to convince him to stay because she will not directly express her desire. To do so would violate the necessary alienation of the public realm and bring her private concern into it.

Captain Wentworth understands the need for indirection as well. Though he does finally communicate his desire to Anne, he does so in a letter he leaves on a table for her, not in a conversation. In the letter, he lets Anne know that he has resorted to this medium because, as he says, "I must speak to you by such means as are within my reach." He asks her to indicate her desire for him not by proclaiming it, but with indirection: "A word, a look, will be enough to decide whether I enter your father's house this evening — or never." Anne is soon able to give Captain Wentworth this look. Immediately after reading the letter, Anne runs into him in the street and gives him the indication — by quietly taking his hand — that she desires him. This gesture is the extent of Anne's expression of love, and yet this absence of direct public expression is what allows her to sustain herself as a subject.

After both Captain Wentworth and Anne have an indication of the other's desire, one would expect to hear them further discourse on their feelings for each other. This may be what happens as they walk away after Anne has given Captain Wentworth her hand, but it is a conversation that the spectator cannot hear. The noise of a passing parade obscures their conversation, leaving their private world still a mystery.[27] This uncertainty surrounding their desires continues into the next scene — the card party at Sir Walter's house. When Captain Wentworth arrives, Mr Elliot is speaking intimately with Anne (a situation which Wentworth misunderstood earlier at the concert). At this point, the spectator is in the situation of a lover — unsure if the Captain and Anne have already reached an understanding or if he will again misrecognize the situation. Captain Wentworth and Anne have already agreed to be married, but by withholding this knowledge from the spectator, the film attempts to create the alienation in the spectator which has plagued Anne and Captain Wentworth throughout the film.[28] We must not fail to recognize the necessity of this alienation. Without it, we lose touch with our subjectivity altogether and become incapable of the love we see on display in *Persuasion*.

By creating a public world, *Persuasion* offers us a picture of how the public works in relation to our alienated subjectivity. When the private becomes ubiquitous and the public loses its distinctiveness, we lose touch with ourselves as subjects. It is in the distance of alienation that subjectivity has an opportunity to find itself. Contemporary Jane Austen films, like her novels, show the importance of sustaining the public not for its own sake but for the space that it offers subjectivity. When we abandon the public to escape alienation, we lose contact with subjectivity at the same moment.[29]

Public Disappearance

The public is a realm of openness that depends on the absence of any external barriers that would generate exclusivity.[30] It forms through an internal barrier that alienates everyone who takes part in it. The absence of external barriers is a barrier to inclusion: there is no way to determine that one is inside, no way to know that one is included. Because it has no exclusivity, the public doesn't enable anyone to view it as their place. A public world in which no one belongs is a more habitable world for everyone. Asserting the right of the public over that of the exclusive community is central to the emancipatory project.

The problem is that the public is constantly endangered. Capitalist society circumscribes the public realm by creating vast expanses of private property that threaten to overrun the public. This society confines the public to parks, libraries, roads, sidewalks, nature preserves, and a few other spaces. One persistent crisis in major cities is the absence of public bathrooms. Private space dominates — it is everywhere one looks — while public space is limited to these sparse areas. This space is uninhabitable in capitalist society, which is why those who live in it are known as *homeless*.[31] To lack a private home, to live in public space, is to lack a home.

When it comes to arenas that make room for debate and political exchanges, there is even less space open to everyone. Most of the forums for political engagement are private rather than public: from discussions in a private home and letters to the newspaper editor to dinner parties and posts on social media, privacy prevails. The public opportunities for political engagement, in contrast, are limited to occasional trips to the voting booth and equally infrequent protests. The private realm dominates politics, despite the fact that political contestation is an inherently public activity concerned with the direction that the society as a whole will take.

The problem with confining the public to these isolated islands within an ocean of privacy is that it has the effect of obscuring the individual subject's relationship to the collective. The shell of privacy comes to appear as the normal state of things, while the openness of the public looks like an exception. Rather than seeing privacy as an interruption of the public, it seems as if the public interrupts the intrinsic dominance of the private. Privacy appears as the natural condition. In this situation, we don't recognize alienation as constitutive of our subjectivity. Instead, we regard it as a possibility that we hope to avoid. According to this way of thinking, it is far better to hide in the apparent safety of one's private community than to venture out into the alienating public realm that represents a fall from the paradise of privacy.[32]

The challenge is to reconceive the public as what traverses even our most private moments. We should see alienation as our inescapable condition. Before we retreat into privacy, the public constitutes us as who we are. The alienation of our public being is the essential fact of subjectivity, a fact that no amount of symbolic status can obviate. The more one seeks to overcome it, the more recalcitrant it becomes. The more one seeks the solace of community, the more one's alienation from that community hits one over the head. Considering oneself as a public being, first and foremost, turns things around. It opens the subject up to the collective. One discovers the singularity of one's subjectivity and the collective basis for this subjectivity through the embrace of the alienating public realm.

There is probably a danger in completely eliminating

private worlds in the name of a universal public, although this danger seems considerably lessened if we consider the public as the realm of unrelenting alienation. Today we live under the opposite threat, that of an all-encroaching privacy that gobbles up more and more public space with every passing day. Privacy is so appealing because it promises that one can be oneself without having to endure an alienating confrontation with the public. But this respite is deceptive. Sinking into privacy always rekindles the spark of alienation.

In a community, we can be with others who share our symbolic identity. But investing oneself in a community is just another way of choosing privacy. When we inhabit a private world, we remain oblivious to the alienation that constitutes our subjectivity. We don't see our failure to be ourselves. Privacy deceives insofar as it insulates us from our dependence on what is foreign to us. To regard oneself as a public being, in contrast, is to confront what one is not as integral to one's being.

Community shields us from those who would challenge our identity. It serves as a protective layer that works to make identity secure. The position that one occupies in a community obscures the problem of subjectivity, while the public brings this problem to the fore. Choosing community over the public appears comfortable, but it traps us in the unfreedom of an oppressive retreat from our alienated subjectivity.[33]

Conclusion
Achieving Common
Unhappiness

Everywhere we look something induces us to escape our alienation. We hear that we should search for a soul mate, do yoga, practice meditation, find the perfect job, relax with friends, or spend more time with our family. This omnipresent encouragement to discover a way out of alienation speaks to the danger that we assume it represents. According to our usual way of thinking, the alienated subject poses a threat to itself, to other people, and to society. Those suffering from alienation might kill themselves, hurt others, or violate the norms of human interaction.

But alienation is not unbearable in itself. It is unbearable when one believes in the possibility of an unalienated state, in a past or a future free from the burden of it. The lure of overcoming alienation entraps subjects in the pursuit of a false possibility that deforms their perspective on existence. Existence becomes the struggle to transcend the obstacles standing in the way of achieving happiness. Unhappiness becomes a state to flee rather than the normal state of existence. Burdened by the image of an unalienated future, one finds oneself fleeing from existence itself. In such a position, there is no possibility for finding satisfaction in the everyday variegations of one's life.

People don't become dangerous because of their alienation but because of their belief that they should be self-identical and are failing to achieve this aim. The danger consists in trying to overcome alienation, not in alienation itself. This attitude creates bullies and oppressive regimes along with killers and murderous societies. If people nourish the hope of getting out of their alienated subjectivity, if they believe this is a real possibility, they will often do whatever it takes to achieve it. The image of a life free from alienation authorizes the violence that would bring this possibility into existence. Accepting the fact that alienation is constitutive of one's subjectivity is a way of struggling against this violence.

Becoming reconciled to one's alienation is not a way of accepting oppression as inevitable. Oppression comes into being through the attempt to overcome alienation. People invest themselves in commodities or devote themselves to communities to find ways to escape their alienated subjectivity. They oppress and exclude others in hopes of foisting their own alienation on someone else. But these pathways do not provide the escape that they promise, which is why those who have a vast number of commodities want more and those who have the most elevated status in a community feel the most insecure. People who join an exclusionary community always experience the other at the gate threatening to undo things. The attempt to escape alienation produces cruelty, bullying, and exclusion on a personal level. Socially, it leads to oppression, reification, and ultimately genocide. Accepting alienation as constitutive provides a way to fight against the damage incurred through the efforts at escaping it.

According to the Marxist playwright Bertolt Brecht, the primary obstacle to the formation of an egalitarian society lies in the failure of people to grasp their own alienation. People live alienated lives, but their consumer goods, their social status, and their family lives obscure this state. Brecht sees it as the role of art to facilitate an encounter with alienation, to make alienation available for conscious experience.

Brecht names his artistic practice the *Verfremdungseffekt* or alienation effect. We should be experiencing alienation in capitalist society, but many factors block this experience. Through the work of art, Brecht wants to use the alienation effect to make alienation palpable. This occurs when a work of art breaks the illusion that what we are presently experiencing is natural. It reveals our alienation by denaturalizing our experience. As Brecht states, "what is involved here is, briefly, a technique of taking the human social incidents to be portrayed and labelling them as something striking, something that calls for explanation, is not to be taken for granted, not just natural."[1] When the natural appears denaturalized, we start to question why we took it as natural in the first place. This process of alienation will lead us ultimately to exit the prison of capitalist society. At least this is Brecht's hope. Grasping one's alienation becomes in his vision the basis for attaining the proper class consciousness.

The first problem with Brecht's conception of alienation in relation to social change is that he dreams of a communist future in which alienation no longer exists. This type of political effort to eliminate alienation has its basis in a failure to recognize that the attempt to eliminate alienation is responsible for oppression in the first place. If a political project seeks a cure for alienation, it will itself necessarily act oppressively. The attempt to cure alienation always entails recourse to oppressive measures. This is what Brecht's politics of the aesthetic fails to take into account.

Contra Brecht, the barrier to social change is not our failure to recognize that we are alienated right now. It lies in our collective belief that there is a place beyond the problem of alienation. Whether it is the commodity, the proper health regime, or a utopian future, the point beyond alienation is an ideological lure that we must cast aside. Whatever social change we make under the spell of this lure risks turning into another nightmare.

Rather than trying to cure alienation, the project of emancipation, if we take it seriously, tries to reconcile us to our alienation, to see alienation itself as freedom. It is only when we embrace alienation that we can move beyond the lure of a self-identical subject and a self-identical society. We produce a society structured around the public rather than around our private communities.

When he first announced the project of psychoanalysis in *Studies on Hysteria* in 1895, Sigmund Freud concluded this book with a pithy articulation of what psychoanalytic treatment hopes to accomplish. It does not aim to give patients happiness or to eliminate the troubles of existence. Its aims are very circumscribed. Freud imagines someone objecting to the inability of psychoanalysis to cure alienation once and for all. In his response to this line of thinking, he insists on limiting the scope of what this treatment promises. As Freud sees it, all that psychoanalysis can do is to transform one's "hysterical misery into common unhappiness."[2] Despite all the changes in Freud's theory in the years that followed this statement, he never went back on this conception of the psychoanalytic intervention. This intervention takes the fundamental alienation of the subject as its point of departure and thus never seeks to transcend the common unhappiness that results from it. The embrace of common unhappiness — the embrace of alienation — is the foundation of egalitarian living and an egalitarian society.

This is a lesson not just for individual therapy but for social or political therapy as well. At their best, efforts at social change are attempts to fight against the escape from alienation that creates an oppressive world. This is what we see at work in great political ruptures like the French Revolution, the Haitian Revolution, the Russian Revolution, the suffragist movement, the US Civil Rights movement, Arab Spring, and Black Lives Matter. These projects fought against oppressive symbolic identities that act as barriers to the experience of alienated subjectivity. They assert the right of alienated subjectivity against the authorized distribution of social places. In each case, the political struggle targets and wants to overthrow a social order that obfuscates alienation.

These projects go awry when they interrupt the affirmation of alienated subjectivity by striving for an unalienated future. This is visible in Napoléon Bonaparte's reinstitution of slavery in the French colonies and in Josef Stalin's Great Purge. In these cases, the revolutionary movements didn't just lose steam. They became their opposite — regimes that refused constitutive alienation in hopes of achieving a self-identical society in the future. The lure of attempting to overcome alienation represents the grave threat that every political project, either personal or societal, must confront.

Avoiding this threat requires changing our relationship to alienation. It involves recognizing how alienation from our family, from our community, and from our nation is what sets us free. No matter how seductive it appears, belonging is always a trap that would steal this freedom and make genuine solidarity impossible. It is only as alienated beings that we can find ourselves where we aren't. It is only as alienated beings that we can experience solidarity with equally alienated others.

Notes

Introduction

1 Death marks the end of alienation because it is the point at which we become completely alien. With death, the subject loses itself into otherness without retaining the least bit of itself.

2 Slavoj Žižek emphasizes the constitutive status of alienation in *Surplus-Enjoyment*. We are not first whole and then alienated but become who we are initially through alienation. This is why he notes that "there is no actual life external to alienation which serves as its positive foundation." Slavoj Žižek, *Surplus Enjoyment: A Guide for the Non-Perplexed* (London: Bloomsbury, 2022), 39. To believe that we exist prior to our alienation is to succumb to a nostalgia for an origin that never existed.

3 Freud pointedly opts for the German term *unbewußt* to describe his conception of the unconscious, rather than the more common, at least at the time, *bewußtlos*. *Bewußtlos* means without consciousness, whereas *unbewußt* signifies what is the opposite of consciousness, something foreign to the structure of consciousness.

4 Freud gives the unconscious structural priority in the psyche. Even though the unconscious, by definition, escapes our conscious control, it plays a larger role in forming who we are than our conscious thinking. In *The Interpretation of Dreams*, Freud states, "The unconscious is the true psychical reality." Sigmund Freud, *The Interpretation of Dreams*, trans. James Strachey, in *The Complete Psychological Works of Sigmund Freud*, vol. 5, ed. James

Strachey (London: Hogarth Press, 1953 [1900]), 651. Even though Freud wrote this early on in his theoretical development, he never wavered on the priority that the unconscious has, even as he moved on from other ideas articulated in *The Interpretation of Dreams*.

5   Jean-Paul Sartre argues that subjectivity is alienated but contends that all other being is fully self-identical. There is, for Sartre, a radical ontological distinction between the subject, which is for-itself, and all other being, which is in-itself. In *Being and Nothingness*, he claims, "Being is. Being is in-itself. Being is what it is." Jean-Paul Sartre, *Being and Nothingness*, trans. Hazel E. Barnes (New York: Washington Square Press, 1956 [1943]), 29. Here, Sartre fails to take into account how the alienated subject might have emerged as alienated. If being were simply what it is, there would be no moment when the subject could break from this pure realm of self-identity.

6   Although I cannot verify it, my mother always claimed that I was one child who did in fact choose its own name. She put several slips of paper in a hat and then placed my newborn hand into the hat. The name on the slip that I first grabbed became my name. The problem with this attempt to avoid imposing an alien name on the child is that the adult establishes the rules of the game. My mother divided up the slips of paper, arranged them in the hat, and ultimately chose which names would be included and which would not be. There is no shortcut around the alienation inhering in the process of naming. Further cementing this point was her confession, albeit after she had developed Alzheimer's disease, that she stacked the deck and wrote *Todd* on every piece of paper. Whether this final admission was true or a delusion created by the disease, it nonetheless reveals how subject the child's name is to the external whims of its guardians.

7   Following predicate or first-order logic, a statement of identity
    does not include difference. To read difference into such a
    statement would be to make a category error, taking one
    sense of the verb *is* for another, confusing identification with
    predication. This is exactly Bertrand Russell's critique of Hegel's
    entire philosophical edifice. For Russell, Hegel wrongly comes
    up with identity in difference — or the subject's fundamental
    alienation — because he fails to see that the statement "Scott is
    the author of *Waverly*" doesn't involve predication but functions
    rather as a statement of identity. For a critique of this position
    and a defense of Hegel, see Todd McGowan, *Emancipation After
    Hegel: Achieving a Contradictory Revolution* (New York: Columbia
    University Press, 2019).

8   Put another way, no one thinks *Paradise Regained* is a greater
    poem than *Paradise Lost*. Alienation is satisfying in a way that
    overcoming it simply isn't. Milton inadvertently demonstrates
    this through the difference in quality between these two works.
    Not only that, but he depicts the figures of nonalienated being in
    Paradise Lost — God, Christ, the angels — as much less appealing
    than Satan, the paradigm of alienation.

9   Not always. Murray Bookchin is one ecologist who, taking Hegel
    as his point of departure, emphasizes the necessity of embracing
    alienation for the ecological project. See Murray Bookchin, *The
    Philosophy of Social Ecology: Essays on Dialectical Naturalism* (Chico:
    AK Press, 2022 [1990]).

Chapter One

1   Jean-Paul Sartre makes this point in his account of the garçon
    de café who acts as if he is a garçon de café. The attempt to
    totally embody a symbolic identity necessarily comes up short.
    As Sartre puts it, "Let us consider this waiter in the cafe. His
    movement is quick and forward, a little too precise, a little too

rapid. He comes toward the patrons with a step a little too quick.
He bends forward a little too eagerly; his voice, his eyes express
an interest a little too solicitous for the order of the customer."
Jean-Paul Sartre, *Being and Nothingness*, trans. Hazel E. Barnes
(New York: Washington Square Press, 1956 [1943]), 59. To really
believe that one is a symbolic identity is, for Sartre, an act of bad
faith, but even the bad faith actor cannot bridge the gap between
subjectivity and symbolic identity. The perfect incorporation is
always too perfect and thus imperfect.

2   The more effort I make to align myself with a symbolic identity,
the more I experience my misalignment with it. This is because
the diligence with which I pursue identification bears witness to
its absence, not its presence. If I really were identical with my
identity as a professor, I wouldn't have to spend so much time
dressing like a professor, talking like a professor, and walking like
a professor.

3   The subject is not Popeye. No subject can legitimately say, "I yam
what I yam."

4   Alenka Zupančič, *What IS Sex?* (Cambridge: MIT Press,
2017), 36.

5   Symbolic identity can itself become a burden in a different way,
especially when it comes with expectations that I'm not inclined
to fulfill. If I have a Jewish symbolic identity, I encounter anti-
Semitism associated with that identity that has nothing to do with
who I am as a subject.

6   Joan Copjec, *Read My Desire: Lacan Against the Historicists*
(Cambridge: MIT Press, 1994), 54–55.

7   In *Blade Runner*, Rick Deckard (Harrison Ford) is a bounty hunter
who pursues fugitive replicants, artificially created beings that
have implanted memories used to domesticate them. Deckard
frees himself from his position as a bounty hunter when he
realizes that his own symbolic identity is just as false as theirs. He

sees how he might be a replicant as well, and even if he's not, he grasps that there is nothing reliable about symbolic identity as such. The film ends with him embarking on a romantic relationship with a woman he knows to be a replicant.

8   Even though these science fiction films reveal an important insight about the alienated status of the subject, the risk inherent in them is that they almost always do so through recourse to paranoia. An external evil imposes the false identity and thereby creates the divide in the subject. We never see this divide resulting from the bare insertion of a being into signification.

9   *Total Recall* doesn't avoid addressing the existential quandary that the absence of any symbolic identity poses for Quaid. When he meets the leader of the revolt of Mars (a mutant named Kuato capable of reading minds), Quaid asks who he is, given that all his memories are false. Like a good student of Jean-Paul Sartre, Kuato responds, "You are what you do. A man is defined by his actions, not his memory." This answer seems to satisfy Quaid, who goes on to play an important role in the revolution that topples the oppressive regime and changes life on Mars.

10   Sigmund Freud, "The Economic Problem of Masochism" (1924), trans. Joan Riviere, in *The Standard Edition of the Complete Psychological Works of Sigmund Freud*, vol. 19, ed. James Strachey (London: Hogarth Press, 1961), 166.

11   Blaise Pascal, *Pensées*, ed. and trans. Roger Ariew (Indianapolis: Hackett, 2005 [1669]), 181.

12   The subject will pay whatever price to sustain its alienation because the greater the price it pays, the more securely it alienates itself. The damage that the subject does to its symbolic identity through self-destructive acts redounds to the benefit of its unconscious desire, which thrives on this damage. The more

a symbolic identity suffers setbacks, the more the unconscious desire of the alienated subject finds itself satisfied.

13   Whereas consciousness rejects what it finds repulsive or what doesn't agree with its values, the unconscious doesn't reject anything. This is a point that Freud brings up in his brief essay "Negation." He claims, "we never discover a 'no' in the unconscious." Sigmund Freud, "Negation" (1925), trans. Joan Riviere, in *The Standard Edition of the Complete Psychological Works of Sigmund Freud*, vol. 19, ed. James Strachey (London: Hogarth Press, 1961), 239. The embrace of everything leads the unconscious to discover what the symbolic structure attempts to keep hidden.

14   In *Being and Time*, Heidegger theorizes silence as secondary to speaking. One can authentically keep silent only when one has something to say. He states, "Keeping silent authentically is possible only in genuine discoursing. To be able to keep silent, Dasein must have something to say." Martin Heidegger, *Being and Time*, trans. John Macquarrie and Edward Robinson (San Francisco: HarperCollins, 1962 [1927]), 154. Heidegger's alignment of silence with authenticity stems from his conviction that silence signifies as much as any use of language.

15   Commentators on subjectivity correctly link its emergence as a philosophical concept to René Descartes, since the *I* plays such an integral part in his thought. His insistence that he can know that he exists because he knows that he is thinking places the problem of subjectivity in the philosophical foreground. That said, he does not use the term *subject* in either *Meditations on First Philosophy* or *Discourse on the Method*, the two major works in which he lays out his philosophical project. Descartes was the discoverer of modern subjectivity because he theorized a divided being capable of taking up an attitude of radical doubt relative to itself. He just lacked the term.

16 Friedrich Nietzsche argues this is a profound misstep on Kant's
    part. For Nietzsche, the subject is just a fiction, not an actual
    entity. Philosophers fall for this fiction, he claims, because they
    allow themselves to be seduced by grammar. The grammatical
    subject leads philosophers to wrongly believe that the subject has
    an ontological weight that it doesn't have. In *Beyond Good and Evil*,
    he asks rhetorically, "Aren't we allowed to be a bit ironic with
    the subject, as we are with the predicate and object? Shouldn't
    philosophers rise above the belief in grammar?" Friedrich
    Nietzsche, *Beyond Good and Evil: Prelude to a Philosophy of the Future*,
    trans. Judith Norman (Cambridge: Cambridge University Press,
    2002 [1885]), 35. What Nietzsche doesn't do is explain how his
    conception of the *Übermensch* escapes the trap that he identifies
    in other thinkers. Shouldn't we be able to reduce Nietzsche's
    own thought to the seductions of grammar and then dismiss its
    truth claims?

17 This is the case solely for those who take up the cause of
    subjectivity. For those critical of the subject, such as Louis
    Althusser, the problem is that it fosters the illusion of self-identity
    and self-mastery. This is the basis for Althusser's critique of
    ideological interpellation, which is the process, he claims, that
    produces subjectivity.

18 If Kant brings the term *subject* into the philosophical mainstream,
    it is the great virtue of Hegel to do the same for *alienation*
    (*Entfremdung*). Although people tend to associate the idea of
    alienation more with Marx than with Hegel, it has a centrality in
    Hegel's thought that it does not have in Marx's.

19 Kant adds a section entitled the "Refutation of Idealism" to the
    second edition of the *Critique of Pure Reason* solely to make sure
    that readers would not mistake his position for Berkeley's.

20 Immanuel Kant, *Critique of Pure Reason*, trans. Paul Guyer and
    Allen W. Wood (Cambridge: Cambridge University Press, 1998
    [1781]), 164.

21 In her landmark study of Kant entitled *Creating the Kingdom of Ends*, Christine Korsgaard insists on the absolute divide between theory and practice in Kantian philosophy. She states, "Reason has two employments, theoretical and practical. We view ourselves as phenomena when we take on the theoretical task of describing and explaining our behavior; we view ourselves as noumena when our practical task is one of deciding what to do. The two standpoints cannot be mixed because these two enterprises — explanation and decision — are mutually exclusive." Christine M. Korsgaard, *Creating the Kingdom of Ends* (Cambridge: Cambridge University Press, 1996), 204. What Korsgaard doesn't add is that this conception of subjectivity as divided between theory and practice is a conception of subjectivity as intrinsically alienated.

22 For Giorgio Agamben, the function of the Nazi death camps was to strip away all political being from those condemned there. The victims of the camp who suffered to the extreme under this power became nothing but biological entities. In *Remnants of Auschwitz*, he lays out his account of the camp as site for the expression of biopower, a power that strips the subject down to its biological functioning so that what is left is just animal being. He writes, "The decisive activity of biopower in our time consists in the production not of life or death, but rather of a mutable and virtually infinite survival." Giorgio Agamben, *Remnants of Auschwitz: The Witness and the Archive*, trans. Daniel Heller-Roazen (New York: Zone Books, 1999 [1998]), 155. This analysis overlooks that the subject can never simply survive, no matter how violently an oppressive power structure operates on it. It remains an alienated — and thus a political — being.

23 Descartes famously hoped that scientific exploration, in contrast to purely speculative philosophy, would help us "to make ourselves, as it were, the lords and masters of nature." René

Descartes, *Discourse on the Method of Rightly Conducting One's Reason and Seeking the Truth in the Sciences*, trans. Robert Stoothoff, in *The Philosophical Writings of Descartes*, vol. 1 (Cambridge: Cambridge University Press, 1985 [1637]), 142–143. Many commentators have pointed out the danger of the attitude toward nature expressed in Descartes' aspiration. This represents a point at which Descartes departs from his own understanding of the subject's dislocation from its world and from itself that he elaborates throughout the *Discourse on the Method*. Earlier in the treatise, Descartes conceives of equality on the basis of the subject's intrinsic alienation from its place of origin.

24 Seeing through the symbolic deception represents another way of avoiding alienation, one that Jennifer Friedlander tackles in *Real Deceptions*. She argues, "As subjects, we must contend with the fundamental deceit of the Symbolic order." Jennifer Friedlander, *Real Deceptions: The Contemporary Reinvention of Realism* (Oxford: Oxford University Press, 2017), 123. The attempt to escape living the lie of the symbolic structure is simultaneously a refusal of alienation. Friedlander's insistence of the necessity of a fundamental deception coincides with an insistence on the necessity of alienation.

25 Aristotle, *Politics*, trans. B. Jowett, in *The Complete Works of Aristotle*, vol. 2, ed. Jonathan Barnes (Princeton: Princeton University Press, 1984), 1278b.

26 Champions of animal liberation tend to have a soft spot for Aristotle. In his view, all living entities exist on the same natural plane. It is this embrace of continuity that renders him a potential ally of animal liberation, in contrast to Plato, who posits a fundamental break between human and animal. Though Aristotle does posit a clear hierarchy among animals (and among humans), he nonetheless grants a soul to animals that modern philosophers would deny.

27 In contrast to Aristotle, when Plato imagines his ideal society,
    he specifically does not include slaves and envisions equality for
    women. Even though Plato installs the philosophers as the ruling
    class in his ideal society, he envisions a society with sexual equality
    and without slaves. His is an ideal that rejects democracy for the
    sake of equality, an equality that Aristotle cannot imagine.

28 Psychoanalysis addresses itself to the subject, not to the human
    animal or the cultural identity that houses this subject. Even if
    Freud himself expresses the hope that someday biological science
    will confirm and build on his insights, this just shows that he
    doesn't understand fully the nature of his own theory. The lasting
    value of psychoanalysis depends on the fact that no scientific
    discovery will ever confirm its validity. To hope for this is to
    abandon the project, even if unwittingly.

29 While there are occasionally subjects who manage to eat healthily,
    avoiding chocolate doughnuts and Twinkies, these outliers do
    not do so naturally. That is, healthy eating is always a response to
    the alternative of unhealthy eating. When opting for spinach in
    lieu of fried Oreos, my mother-in-law finds satisfaction in giving
    up what is unhealthy rather than directly in the consumption of
    the healthy. There is no unalienated relationship to eating for the
    alienated subject.

30 This is how Freud defines sexual perversion, although he insists
    at the same time that we cannot use it as a critique, precisely
    because it is nearly ubiquitous in human sexuality. He writes,
    "Perversions are sexual activities which either (*a*) extend, in
    an anatomical sense, beyond the regions of the body that are
    designed for sexual union, or (*b*) linger over the immediate
    relations to the sexual object which should normally be traversed
    rapidly on the path towards the final sexual aim." Sigmund
    Freud, *Three Essays on the Three of Sexuality*, in *The Standard
    Edition of the Complete Psychological Works of Sigmund Freud*, vol. 7,

trans. and ed. James Strachey (London: Hogarth Press, 1953 [1905]),149–150.

31 Daniel Lieberman, *The Story of the Human Body: Evolution, Heath, and Disease* (New York: Pantheon, 2013), 16.

32 Steven Pinker, *How the Mind Works* (New York: Norton, 1997), 473. Pinker claims that this adaptation for promiscuity is confined completely to men and that women have little genetic interest at all in multiple partners. But fellow evolutionary psychologist David Buss counters by noting the adaptive benefits of affairs for women. He states, "The economics of the mating market dictate that women can secure genes from an affair partner that are superior to those of her regular partner, at least in principle. A highly desirable man is often willing to have a brief encounter with a less desirable woman, as long as she does not burden him with entangling commitments. Indeed, if there were no costs, an optimal female mating strategy, in the ruthless currency of reproductive fitness, would be to secure reliable investments from her husband and superior genes from an affair partner." David Buss, *The Evolution of Desire: Strategies of Human Mating*, rev. ed. (New York: Basic Books, 2003 [1994]), 235–236. The problem with each of these arguments lies in the fact that the only way one can decide between them is on the basis of their political desirability. A contemporary Kantian might even say that these opposed arguments reveal the antinomies of naturalist reason.

33 See — or not — Randy Thornhill and Craig T. Palmer, *A Natural History of Rape: Biological Bases of Sexual Coercion* (Cambridge: MIT Press, 2000).

34 Peter B. Gray, "Evolution and Human Sexuality," *Yearbook of Physical Anthropology* 152 (2013): 20.

35 Grasping alienation as constitutive for oneself as a subject is what Hegel, in the *Phenomenology of Spirit*, calls absolute knowing. By achieving this, one finds oneself at home in what is alien.

Or, as Hegel puts it, for the spirit that attains absolute knowing, "in *its* otherness as such, it is at one with itself." G. W. F. Hegel, *Phenomenology of Spirit*, trans. Terry Pinkard (Cambridge: Cambridge University Press, 2018 [1807]), 454. To be at home in one's otherness is to make a home out of the constitutive alienation of subjectivity, to embrace being out of place as one's only possible relationship to place. Doing so requires becoming comfortable with being uncomfortable. Only by accomplishing this can we sustain the problem of subjectivity without rushing toward a solution that will always makes matters worse.

Chapter Two

1   In his famous history of modern science, E. A. Burtt points out that Galileo's system specifically displaces the human from its former position. In this system, according to Burtt, "The natural world was portrayed as a vast, self-contained mathematical machine, consisting of motions of matter in space and time, and man with his purposes, feelings, and secondary qualities was shoved apart as an unimportant spectator and semi-real effect of the great mathematical drama outside." E. A. Burtt, *The Metaphysical Foundations of Modern Science* (Mineola: Dover, 2003 [1924]), 104. Modern science leaves subjectivity aside in order to make sense of the universe.

2   This displacement of Earth from the center of the world is the decisive modern event. For this reason, Steven Weinberg is certainly right to contend, "Whatever the scientific revolution was or was not, it began with Copernicus." Steven Weinberg, *To Explain the World: The Discovery of Modern Science* (New York: HarperCollins, 2015), 147. Although Copernicus did not suffer for his beliefs in the way that later scientists such as Giordano Bruno and Galileo Galilei did, his breakthrough was the founding gesture of modernity.

3   Humanity's place at the center of creation is not a privilege
     for premodern thinking. For Aristotle, the celestial spheres that
     encircle Earth and the prime mover beyond them are the realms
     of perfection. The circular motion of the spheres testifies to this
     perfection, while Earth's sublunary status reveals its imperfection.
     For Christian thinkers following Aristotle, the position of Earth in
     the world corresponds to humanity's debased status relative to the
     rest of creation.

4   It was actually Copernicus's spouse who pushed him toward the
     discovery of heliocentrism. Copernicus developed his theory
     after a series of domestic quarrels about their offspring. His wife
     triangulated with him and put the son in the middle of their
     disputes. After contemplating the structure of this method of
     arguing, Copernicus recognized its astronomical implications.

5   Giordano Bruno, *Cause, Principle, and Unity*, trans. and ed. Robert
     De Lucca (Cambridge: Cambridge University Press, 2004
     [1584]), 87.

6   Arthur Lovejoy compellingly argues that Bruno played a more
     significant role than Copernicus in the modern uprooting
     of humanity. He states, "it is Giordano Bruno who must be
     regarded as the principal representative of the doctrine of the
     decentralized, infinite, and infinitely populous universe; for he
     not only preached it throughout Western Europe with the fervor
     of an evangelist, but also first gave a thorough statement of the
     grounds on which it was to gain acceptance from the general
     public." Arthur O. Lovejoy, *The Great Chain of Being: A Study of the
     History of an Idea* (Cambridge: Harvard University Press, 1936),
     116. Bruno's commitment to the infinite disrupts the ability to
     think of humanity as localizable. In an infinite universe, the idea
     of a center eventually ceases to have any significance at all.

7   Alexandre Koyré, *From the Closed World to the Infinite Universe*
     (Baltimore: Johns Hopkins University Press, 1957), 78.

8   Spartacus does not lead a slave revolt in the name of universal
    freedom. The predominance of place in the Roman world made
    such a value, even for the revolting slave, unthinkable. But in
    modern Haiti, freedom functioned as the watchword of the
    Haitian slave revolt.

9   There is a conception of freedom in ancient Hinduism, but it is
    not the freedom to act. It is the freedom from action. According
    to the *Bhagavad Gita*, "One who is free from selfish attachments,
    who has mastered himself and his passions, attains the supreme
    perfection of freedom from action." *Bhagavad Gita*, trans. Eknath
    Easwaran (Tomales: Nilgiri Press, 1985), 18:49. Millenia after
    the writing of the *Bhagavad Gita*, Mahatma Gandhi would
    make freedom from action into the basis for political freedom.
    Although Gandhi theorized his revolt through the *Bhagavad Gita*,
    it was a thoroughly modern phenomenon insofar as it challenged
    the constraints of social place.

10 In *Theory of the Subject*, Alain Badiou defines the ruling class by its
    commitment to the stability of place. He writes, "A ruling class
    is the guardian of the place." Alain Badiou, *Theory of the Subject*,
    trans. Bruno Bosteels (New York: Continuum, 2009 [1982]),
    184. Modernity is the epoch of revolutionary tumults because it
    inaugurates a challenge to place.

11 Frantz Fanon, *Black Skin, White Masks*, trans. Richard Philcox
    (New York: Grove Press, 2008 [1952]), 204–205.

12 The great virtue of David Graeber and David Wengrow's *The
    Dawn of Everything* is that it exposes how modernity was not
    simply a European project. The great ideas of modernity —
    freedom, equality, and solidarity — emerged through dialogue
    with other peoples, who often had more enlightened views on
    these questions than their European interlocutors. What Graeber
    and Wengrow don't do is link these values to alienation or
    recognize any virtue in alienation at all. That said, their book is

like a breath of fresh air in the face of most evolutionary histories of humanity. See David Graeber and David Wengrow, *The Dawn of Everything: A New History of Humanity* (New York: Farrar, Straus and Giroux, 2021).

13 Marx grasps perfectly the relationship that we should take up to tradition in *The Eighteenth Brumaire of Louis Bonaparte*. Toward the beginning of this work, he states, "The tradition of the dead generations weighs like a nightmare on the minds of the living." Karl Marx, *The Eighteenth Brumaire of Louis Bonaparte*, in *Political Writings, Volume 2: Surveys from Exile* (London: Verso, 2010 [1852]), 146. Marx's political vision rightly includes a necessary break from tradition. He recognizes that tradition is always unfreedom, no matter how comfortable it feels to us.

14 When Hamlet first appears, we see his distance from the current ruling authority in Denmark, his uncle Claudius. While everyone else celebrates, Hamlet remains aloof and insists on his distance from Claudius and his mother, who has married him.

15 Antigone's absolute certainty and lack of self-doubt is evident from the first scene of *Antigone*. In this scene, she makes no allowance for the legitimate questions that her sister Ismene poses. Instead, after Antigone briefly lays out the situation for Ismene, she states categorically, "That is the new trouble. And now you can prove / who you are: good sister or coward / and disgrace to our brave ancestors." Sophocles, *Antigone*, in *The Theban Plays of Sophocles*, trans. David R. Slavitt (New Haven: Yale University Press, 2007), 3. Hamlet not only permits questions from others but bombards himself with them in a way that would be unthinkable in an ancient hero such as Antigone.

16 Once one accepts the hypothesis of a delay, Sigmund Freud offers the most convincing explanation for it. His interpretation, developed initially in a footnote to *The Interpretation of Dreams*, receives a fuller treatment in Ernest Jones, *Hamlet and Oedipus*

(New York: Norton, 1976 [1949]). According to Freud and Jones, Hamlet delays because he unconsciously desires to do what Claudius has done — namely, to kill his father and have sex with his mother.

17 In an essay that recognizes Hamlet's act taking place throughout the play, Walter Davis argues that the entirety of the play consists in Hamlet attacking Claudius (and every other character) psychically to force them to confront the trauma of their own subjectivity. Davis states, "Shakespeare put in the soliloquy [when Hamlet refrains from killing Claudius ...] so that even the groundlings in academe would see what Hamlet has been doing all along, torturing everyone psychologically, murdering people the way his true successor Iago does, by planting poison in their psyches then watching it work." Walter A. Davis, "Beyond Humanism and Postmodernism: A *Hamlet* for the 21st Century," in *Shakespeare After 9/11: How a Social Trauma Reshapes Interpretation*, eds. Matthew Biberman and Julia Reinhard Lupton (Lewiston: Edward Mellen Press, 2011), 280.

18 William Shakespeare, *The Tragedy of Hamlet, Prince of Denmark*, in *The Riverside Shakespeare*, 2nd ed., ed. G. Blakemore Evans (Boston: Houghton Mifflin, 1997 [1600]), act 1, scene 5, lines 188–189.

19 One could imagine an alternate ending of *Hamlet* in which the ghost appeared on the stage with a satisfied look on his face just after the death of Claudius. If George Lucas had written *Hamlet*, this would surely have been the result, mirroring the miraculous appearance of the ghosts of Obi-Wan Kenobi (Alec Guinness), Yoda (Frank Oz), and Anakin Skywalker (Sebastian Shaw) at the conclusion of Richard Marquand's *Return of the Jedi* (1983).

20 William Shakespeare, *The Tragedy of Othello, the Moor of Venice*, in *The Riverside Shakespeare*, 2nd ed., ed. G. Blakemore Evans (Boston: Houghton Mifflin, 1997 [1604]), act 2, scene 3, lines 351–353.

21 Shakespeare, *Othello*, act 5, scene 2, lines 355–356.

22 Hannah Arendt famously labels Adolf Eichmann's brand
    of evil banal in her *Eichmann in Jerusalem*. While she is surely
    wrong to take at face value Eichmann's claim that he was just
    a party functionary with no animus toward Jews, we can see
    in her insistence on the banality of his evil a political effort to
    bar Eichmann from reaching the status of Iago or Vautrin (in
    Honoré de Balzac's *Père Goriot*). Arendt states, "It was sheer
    thoughtlessness — something by no means identical with
    stupidity — that predisposed him to become one of the greatest
    criminals of that period." Hannah Arendt, *Eichmann in Jerusalem:
    A Report on the Banality of Evil* (New York: Penguin, 2006 [1963]).
    287–288. For Arendt, to categorize Eichmann as a figure of
    diabolical evil is to credit Nazism with a transcendence that it
    cannot achieve.

23 Immanuel Kant, *Religion within the Boundaries of Mere Reason*,
    in *Religion within the Boundaries of Mere Reason and Other Writings*,
    trans. and ed. Allen Wood and George di Giovanni (New York:
    Cambridge University Press, 1996 [1793]), 82.

24 Alenka Zupančič contends that Kant disallows diabolical evil to
    protect his own version of morality. According to Zupančič, the
    Kantian moral act is formally indistinguishable from diabolical
    evil. In *Ethics of the Real*, she writes, "Following Kant — but at
    the same time going against Kant — we thus propose to assert
    explicitly that *diabolical evil, the highest evil, is indistinguishable from
    the highest good, and that they are nothing other than the definitions of an
    accomplished (ethical) act.* In other words, at the level of the structure
    of the ethical act, the difference between good and evil does not
    exist. At this level, evil is formally indistinguishable from good."
    Alenka Zupančič, *Ethics of the Real: Kant, Lacan* (London: Verso,
    2000), 92.

25 What Lear says that he wants, "To shake all cares and business from our age," is impossible for the speaking subject. William Shakespeare, *The Tragedy of King Lear*, in *The Riverside Shakespeare*, 2nd ed., ed. G. Blakemore Evans (Boston: Houghton Mifflin, 1997 [1606]), act 1, scene 1, line 39. The subject cannot exempt itself from cares because it is always outside of itself in the world that it inhabits.

26 Shakespeare, *King Lear*, act 1, scene 1, line 62.

27 Shakespeare, *King Lear*, act 1, scene 1, lines 91–93.

28 It is the explicit alienation from traditional authority that makes Descartes the first modern philosopher. Michel de Montaigne, his chief competitor for this title, does not emphasize the rupture.

29 René Descartes, *Discourse on the Method of Rightly Conducting One's Reason and Seeking the Truth in the Sciences*, trans. Robert Stoothoff, in *The Philosophical Writings of Descartes*, vol. 1 (Cambridge: Cambridge University Press, 1985 [1637]), 115.

30 René Descartes, *Meditations on First Philosophy*, trans. John Cottingham (Cambridge: Cambridge University Press, 1986 [1641]), 12.

31 Descartes, *Discourse on the Method*, 118.

32 Although Heidegger refuses the subject that Kant embraces, Hegel is Heidegger's primary opponent. He has much more fondness for Kant because Hegel so unabashedly extols the emancipatory power of subjectivity. Kant introduces the term into philosophy, but Hegel turns it into the first word in the philosophical lexicon of modernity.

33 Martin Heidegger, *Being and Time*, trans. John Macquarrie and Edward Robinson (San Francisco: HarperCollins, 1962 [1927]), 367.

34 Martin Heidegger, *Kant and the Problem of Metaphysics*, 5th ed., trans. Richard Taft (Bloomington: Indiana University Press, 1997 [1929]), 160.

35 Heidegger, *Being and Time*, 222.

36 In his insightful account of Heidegger's philosophical project, Jeff Malpas states, "human being is essentially a being in place, just as it is also a being in the world." Jeff Malpas, *Heidegger and the Thinking of Place: Explorations in the Topology of Being* (Cambridge: MIT Press, 2012), 63. Here, Malpas links Heidegger's sense of Dasein as a being in the world with a place for Dasein.

37 Heidegger articulates the appeal of National Socialism for him in a published work, *Introduction to Metaphysics*, where he identifies what he sees as "the inner truth and greatness of this movement" — the way that Nazism confronts "the encounter between global technology and modern humanity." Martin Heidegger, *Introduction to Metaphysics*, 2nd ed., trans. Gregory Fried and Richard Polt (New Haven: Yale University Press, 2014 [1953]), 222. Heidegger sees in Nazism the promise of engaging with modernity by restoring a sense of place that modernity strips away. The party's nationalism, promotion of Aryan identity, and ruthlessness toward its enemies are part of the bargain.

38 Although Heidegger is one of the parent figures of existentialism, his antimodernity definitively separates him from Jean-Paul Sartre and Simone de Beauvoir. Sartre and Beauvoir embrace modernity to such an extent that they assert themselves as the fellow travelers of communism, a position that Heidegger definitively rejects as symptomatic of modern homelessness.

39 The original version of *Battlestar Galactica* ran for only one season (1978–1979). The new series keeps most of the same characters from the original but often introduces changes as well. About the original series, the less said, the better.

40 In the aftermath of the September 11th attack on the United States, the show presents its heroes, the humans, as rebels who resort to terrorist acts and even suicide bombings when they find themselves captured by the Cylons.

41 *Battlestar Galactica* is one of the few series destroyed by its ending. Had it ended on the desolate planet Earth rather than going on to a new Earth, there would be an argument that it was the best television series ever made. The ending provides a definitive refutation of this argument.

Chapter Three

1 For Jürgen Habermas, what appear as the evils of modernity are actually the result of the failure to finish the project of modernity. In "Modernity and Postmodernity," Habermas takes on the various strains of antimodern critique, from the traditional conservative to the neoconservative to the sophistic leftist. He states, "I think that instead of giving up modernity and its project as a lost cause, we should learn from the mistakes of those extravagant programs which have tried to negate modernity." Jürgen Habermas, "Modernity versus Postmodernity," trans. Seyla Benhabib, *New German Critique* 22 (1981): 11. While Habermas is certainly correct to reject what he calls postmodernity (by which he means the leftist philosophers taking their lead from Friedrich Nietzsche and Martin Heidegger), he undersells the extent to which the evils of modernity are really the evils of modernity. Stalinism, for instance, cannot just be chalked up to the victory of antimodern forces. It emerges from an attempt to modernize at all costs. That said, Habermas's sense that we need more modernity to counteract these evils, not less, is surely on the right track.

2 Bruno Latour struggles against the horrors of modernity not by taking up an antimodern position but by refusing to acknowledge the modern break at all. For Latour, modernity is just another tradition. See Bruno Latour, *We Have Never Been Modern*, trans. Catherine Porter (Cambridge: Harvard University Press, 1993 [1991]).

3   This is the case with Paul Tibbets, who dropped the first atomic
     bomb on the city of Hiroshima. For the definitive account of the
     psychic underpinnings of this event (including those of Tibbets
     himself), see Walter A. Davis, *The Holocaust Memorial: A Play about
     Hiroshima* (Bloomington: 1st Books, 2000).

4   The problem with Steven Pinker's claim in *The Better Angels of
     Our Nature* that the modern universe is much less violent than
     the premodern world is that he writes mass violence out of the
     equation. It is true that a European city in 2020 is much safer
     than the same city in 1520, but this increased safety depends
     on structural violence that the dweller in this city cannot see.
     It relies on minerals mined under horrific conditions in the
     Congo or elsewhere, proxy wars fought around the globe, and
     a tightly patrolled border, to name just its most conspicuous
     manifestations. Modernity makes violence less visible, but
     it doesn't minimize it. This violence is the way that modern
     subjects retreat from the trauma of modernity that makes their
     transcendental homelessness visible.

5   In addition to multiplying the scale of violent acts, modernity
     offers the possibility for evading these acts psychically. One can
     act violently while at the same time denying the reality of this
     act to oneself. Sigmund Freud's name for this psychic operation
     is fetishistic disavowal. Even though we can imagine fetishistic
     disavowal operating in the premodern world, it becomes
     mainstream with modernity.

6   Max Horkheimer and Theodor W. Adorno, *Dialectic of
     Enlightenment: Philosophical Fragments*, trans. Edmund Jephcott
     (Stanford: Stanford University Press, 2002 [1947]), 211.

7   Although she opposes herself vehemently to Adorno both
     theoretically and personally, Hannah Arendt shares Adorno
     and Horkheimer's critique of the alienation that modernity
     brings to the fore. Their agreement on this question reveals just

how far the critical consensus goes. In *Origins of Totalitarianism*, Arendt writes, "What prepares men for totalitarian domination in the non-totalitarian world is the fact that loneliness, once a borderline experience usually suffered in certain marginal social conditions like old age, has become an everyday experience of the evergrowing masses of our century. The merciless process into which totalitarianism drives and organizes the masses looks like a suicidal escape from this reality." Hannah Arendt, *The Origins of Totalitarianism* (New York: Harcourt, 1968 [1951]), 478. According to this view, the lonely alienation of the modern subject paves the way for totalitarianism.

8   Sometimes oppressive forces openly discuss reducing the targets of their oppression to the status of mere beasts (or even lice). But even the most oppressive situation cannot do away with the divided subject or the unconscious of the oppressed. There has never been a successful oppressive situation, if we take the stated goal as the true aim. Even the oppressors have an unconscious and desire something other than what they say they want.

9   Here, we should think about the way Rassemblement National approaches Muslim immigrants in France. From this political party's perspective, these immigrants cannot be alienated subjects, even though one might imagine living as a Muslim in today's France would be alienating, given the prejudice that one must endure. Instead, for this rightist party, the desire of Muslim immigrants is clear: they repudiate French *laïcité* (the national policy that religion should not intrude on the public arena), deny the equality of women, want to impose Sharia law on the nation, and destroy the country's Catholic heritage. This oppressive viewpoint does not permit Muslim immigrants their alienation — their mixed desires relative to laïcité, enforced equality, and France. Oppression sees its targets as figures fully identified with their identity. Immigrants are nothing but immigrants. None

has any desire that transcends the identity attributed to the immigrant.

10 In other words, the struggle for an authentic individual existence and the struggle for equality are fundamentally the same. To forget either about the alienation of the subject or the alienation of society is to abandon implicitly the other struggle.

11 In the final lines of his first novel *Sister Carrie*, Theodore Dreiser describes the situation of capitalist subjectivity. As the events of the novel come to a close, Carrie Meeber finds herself still striving for more, despite the social climbing that she has accomplished during the course of the narrative. The novel's narrator describes a situation that Carrie herself does not grasp. The narrator comments on Carrie's position by addressing her, "In your rocking-chair, by your window dreaming, shall you long, alone. In your rocking-chair, by your window, shall you dream such happiness as you may never feel." Theodore Dreiser, *Sister Carrie* (New York: Bantam, 1982 [1900]), 400.

12 Adam Smith argues that capitalism reconciles the individual with the social order as a whole. Individuals pursue their own self-interest, but this self-interest, when considered logically, ends up coinciding with that of the society. As Smith puts it, "Every individual is continually exerting himself to find out the most advantageous employment for whatever capital he can command. It is his own advantage, indeed, and not that of society, which he has in view. But the study of his own advantage naturally, or rather necessarily, leads him to prefer that employment which is most advantageous to society." Adam Smith, *An Inquiry into the Nature and Causes of the Wealth of Nations* (Hamburg: Management Laboratory Press, 2008 [1776]), 343–344. The most obvious marker of the subject's alienation — its disjunction with the social order in which it exists — disappears in Smith's rendering of how capitalism works. Of course, the

theory of capitalism is not its practice. But this theory indicates how subjects experience the practice of capitalism. It functions in a way that hides our alienation by telling us that our desires fit with what the social order requires of us.

13 Karl Marx, *Grundrisse*, trans. Martin Nicolaus (New York: Penguin, 1993 [1857–1858]), 92.

14 One of the great virtues of the television series *Succession* is that it makes clear just how much those who win the capitalist game fail to find it satisfying. No cognizant spectator would ever dream of changing places with anyone in the Roy family or the people from their socioeconomic cohort. As capitalism's winners, everyone in the series must commit themselves to overcoming alienation, no matter what the cost to their relationships.

15 The impact of racism extends through every aspect of modernity. One cannot separate, for instance, the development of capitalism from racism, since slavery plays such a crucial role in making capitalism possible. Even if capitalism eventually does without chattel slavery and confines itself to paid labor, the accumulation necessary for the development of capitalism is unthinkable without this initial period of slave labor.

16 Despite the stark disagreements between Kant and the utilitarian philosophers, both sides reject the morality of slave society. They do so for different reasons, but they nonetheless share the belief that it runs contrary to morality. For Kant, it violates the moral law by reducing a subject to a pure means to an end, whereas for someone like John Stuart Mill, it is incompatible with the pursuit of the greatest possible happiness for all.

17 Frantz Fanon, *The Wretched of the Earth*, trans. Richard Philcox (New York: Grove Press, 2004 [1961]), 236.

18 In *Orientalism*, Edward Said points out that the primary gesture of Orientalism (akin to all racism) lies in depriving the other of any self-division. He writes, "The Oriental is given as fixed,

stable, in need of investigation, in need even of knowledge about himself. No dialectic is either desired or allowed." Edward Said, *Orientalism* (New York: Vintage, 1978), 308. Orientalism creates a stable opposition where the racial other exists in a fixed symbolic position. The key to this equation is that this other must not have any unconscious desire that would disrupt the consistency of the symbolic position. The outbreak of unconscious desire would attest to the failure of the racist project.

19 As Achille Mbembe points out, "The notion of race made it possible to represent non-European human groups as trapped in a lesser form of being. They were the impoverished reflection of the ideal man, separated from him by an insurmountable temporal divide, a difference nearly impossible to overcome." Achille Mbembe, *Critique of Black Reason*, trans. Laurent Dubois (Durham: Duke University Press, 2017 [2013]), 17.

20 It is fashionable today to make reference to race while at the same time distancing oneself from the existence of biological races. One acknowledges that race is a cultural construct and not a biological fact. This is a position that the Fields sisters appropriately shoot down. They write, "Race as culture is only biological race in polite language: No one can seriously postulate cultural homogeneity among those who racial homogeneity scholars nonetheless take for granted." Karen E. Fields and Barbara J. Fields, *Racecraft: The Soul of Inequality in American Life* (London: Verso, 2012), 156. To invoke race as a cultural fact is to participate in the mystification of racism just as much as when one invokes race as a biological fact.

21 Fields and Fields, *Racecraft*, 149.

22 Paul Gilroy, *Against Race: Imagining Political Culture Beyond the Color Line* (Cambridge: Harvard University Press, 2000), 237.

23 The concept of the *working mother* reveals the extent of the identification of women with the home. Even when she works

outside the home, this external employment remains an adjective affixed to a woman's identity and not an essential part of that identity. The man who stays home to take care of the children, in contrast, becomes *Mr Mom*, suggesting that he is not at home in the home but rather becomes feminine when taking up this position.

24   One of Toni Morrison's central fictional projects is exposing how patriarchal figures impede women's encounter with their own alienation. This activity limits how women can revolt against patriarchy. Morrison's novel *Paradise* begins with the forces of sexism attacking a group of women who refuse to stay in their place. A group of five women live at a place known as the Convent. They provide refuge for local women who face domestic abuse, offer abortions for unwanted pregnancies, and generally assist in the struggle against the oppressiveness of patriarchal control. The men of the town of Ruby slaughter the women at the beginning of the novel because they embrace their alienation and encourage other women to do so through their activities. By centering the novel on this act of violence, Morrison reveals how sexist society fears the alienation of women.

25   Simone de Beauvoir, *The Second Sex*, trans. Constance Borde and Sheila Malovany-Chevallier (New York: Vintage, 2011 [1949]), 643.

26   For Beauvoir, it is crucial not to identify sexual oppression with biological determination. This is why she insists that "one is not born, but rather becomes, woman." She adds, "No biological, psychic, or economic destiny defines the figure that the human female takes on in society." Beauvoir, *The Second Sex*, 283.

27   Betty Friedan, *The Feminine Mystique* (New York: Norton, 2013 [1963]), 35–36.

28   Friedan spends a great deal of time in *The Feminine Mystique* blaming Freud for the development of the mystique because

he convinced women that their problems have psychic rather than social causes. She writes, "The feminine mystique derived its power from Freudian thought; for it was an idea born of Freud, which led women, and those who studied them, to misinterpret their mothers' frustrations, and their fathers' and brothers' and husbands' resentments and inadequacies, and their own emotions and possible choices in life. It is a Freudian idea, hardened into apparent fact, that has trapped so many American women today." Friedan, *Feminine Mystique*, 110. While it is true that psychoanalytic practice, especially in the United States, often perpetuated the misleading type of analysis that Friedan reacts against, Freud stands out for his critique of masculinity as imposture. He diagnoses the phallus as always fraudulent. For more on this understanding of psychoanalysis, see Alenka Zupančič, *The Odd One In: On Comedy* (Cambridge: MIT Press, 2008).

Chapter Four

1   Most doctrinaire Marxists today never mention alienation at all. David Harvey, for instance, lays out the problem of capitalism's self-perpetuation not in terms of the problem of alienation but rather those of economic growth. In *The Enigma of Capital and the Crisis of Capitalism*, he writes, "No matter what innovation or shift occurs, the survival of capitalism in the long run depends on the capacity to achieve 3 percent compound growth." David Harvey, *The Enigma of Capital and the Crisis of Capitalism* (Oxford: Oxford University Press, 2010), 130. According to a Marxist such as Harvey, alienation is neither here nor there when it comes to the struggle against capitalism. The fundamental — and interlinked — problems are growth, debt, and finance.

2   Perhaps no follower takes up Marx's critique of Hegel's idealism more pointedly than Theodor Adorno, despite Adorno's own

theoretical sympathy with Hegel. For instance, in a series of lectures entitled *History and Freedom*, Adorno claims that Hegel "really wants to include everything, even things that simply cannot be reconciled. By this I mean that he adopts the standpoint of the universal; he tends always to claim, ideologically and in a conformist spirit, that the universal is in the right." Theodor W. Adorno, *History and Freedom*, trans. Rodney Livingstone (Malden, MA: Polity, 2006 [1964–1965]), 65. Always taking the side of the universal is, for Adorno, his way of refusing the primacy of the material, which he theorizes as the remainder.

3   Karl Marx, "Postface to the Second Edition," in *Capital: A Critique of Political Economy, Volume I*, trans. Ben Fowkes (New York: Penguin, 1976 [1867]), 103. As Marx and Friedrich Engels pithily put it in *The German Ideology*, "It is not consciousness that determines life, but life that determines consciousness." Karl Marx and Friedrich Engels, *The German Ideology* (Moscow: Progress Publishers, 1976 [1845–1846]), 42. When one turns Hegel right-side up, one arrives at this formula.

4   A number of Marxists contrast Hegel's philosophizing with Marx's political program. This group ranges from those more hostile to Hegel, such as Étienne Balibar, to those very friendly to him, such as Frank Ruda.

5   In his one published work devoted specifically to politics, Hegel makes clear in the preface that he doesn't want to offer a theory of how society should be organized. In the *Philosophy of Right*, he states, "This treatise… in so far as it deals with political science, shall be nothing other than an attempt *to comprehend and portray the state as an inherently rational entity*. As a philosophical composition, it must distance itself as far as possible from the obligation to construct a *state as it ought to be*; such instruction as it may contain cannot be aimed at instructing the state on how it ought to be, but rather at showing how the state, as the ethical universe,

should be recognized." G. W. F. Hegel, *Elements of the Philosophy of Right*, trans. H. B. Nisbet, ed. Allen W. Wood (Cambridge: Cambridge University Press, 1991 [1821]), 21. Although Hegel's statement seems to clearly disdain any political bearing in philosophy, it should be said that he places a great deal of political importance on how we do recognize the state, which is, for him, the task of philosophy.

6   G. W. F. Hegel, *Phenomenology of Spirit*, trans. Terry Pinkard (Cambridge: Cambridge University Press, 2018 [1807]), 284.

7   In the *Phenomenology of Spirit*, Hegel praises alienation as the force that creates subjectivity through the destruction of our natural being. He states, "The individual's true *original nature* and his substance are the spirit of the *alienation* of *natural* being." Hegel, *Phenomenology of Spirit*, 285.

8   Hegel insists on the totality and the whole to make clear that alienation cannot be avoided. By stopping short of the totality in our thinking, we leave space that might potentially be free from alienation. Totalizing eliminates this potentiality, which is why it is a radical step.

9   The difference between the *Phenomenology of Spirit* and the *Science of Logic* is that the former traces the alienation of the subject while the latter follows the contradiction of the concept. The *Phenomenology* confines its thinking about contradiction to the subject's alienation.

10   Like Hegel, Marx uses two different terms for alienation, *Entäußerung* and *Entfernung*. Typically, translators use the English word *estrangement* to translate the latter.

11   This is a central preoccupation of the *Economic and Philosophical Manuscripts of 1844*, which a young Marx wrote while in Paris. According to Marx, "the object which labor produces — labor's product — confronts it as *something alien*, as a *power independent* of the producer." Karl Marx, *The Economic and Philosophic Manuscripts*

of 1844, trans. Martin Milligan (New York: International Publishers, 1964 [1844]), 108.

12 Marx, *Economic and Philosophic Manuscripts*, 114.

13 Bertell Ollman links Marx's conception of alienation to the unalienated communist future. This future provides a measure by which we can determine our contemporary alienated status. Ollman writes, "it follows from the acceptance of communism as the relevant measure that all classes are considered alienated in the ways and to the degree that their members fall short of the communist ideal." Bertell Ollman, *Alienation: Marx's Conception of Man in Capitalist Society*, 2nd ed. (Cambridge: Cambridge University Press, 1976 [1971]), 132. Although Ollman avoids positing an original essence that capitalist alienation disturbs, he nonetheless envisions the project of emancipation as one in which we overcome alienation — or at least attempt to do so. This is the relationship to alienation that plays the central role for most emancipatory projects in Marx's aftermath.

14 Descartes provides an initial formulation of alienated subjectivity without using either term. Kant adds the term *subject*. Hegel squares the circles by adding the term *alienation*.

15 Hegel, *Phenomenology of Spirit*, 54.

16 One should imagine that Hegel's target when he theorizes education as a process of alienation to which the child must submit is Jean-Jacques Rousseau's *Emile*. In this foundational work in educational theory, Rousseau sees education as the development of the child's natural tendencies, not a violent imposition of what is alien to the child's nature.

17 Needless to say, Hegel would find home schooling to be an educational catastrophe, a path for depriving children of the possibility for discovering their freedom. Home schooling imagines education without alienation, which is a way of not imagining education at all.

18 In his late *Lectures on the Philosophy of Spirit*, Hegel states, "Something alien is introduced into children, and they as human beings have the presentiment that such rupture is necessary. The alien and strange is the first lesson; reading and writing, abstract tones and signs are the elementary lessons, although in and by themselves [they may be] entirely without spirit. This purely external totality is what they must occupy themselves with." G. W. F. Hegel, *Lectures on the Philosophy of Spirit, 1827-8*, trans. Robert R. Williams (Oxford: Oxford University Press, 2007), 97–98. Hegel recognizes the necessity for an alienating education process that provides the basis for the freedom of subjectivity.

19 G. W. F. Hegel, *The Science of Logic*, trans. George Di Giovanni (Cambridge: Cambridge University Press, 2010 [1812]), 639.

20 Shlomo Avineri, *Hegel's Theory of the Modern State* (Cambridge: Cambridge University Press, 1972), 94. One cannot praise Avineri's book highly enough.

21 Although Herbert Marcuse tries to give his brand of Marxism a Hegelian flavor, he doesn't go far enough in this direction. His political philosophy remains committed to the possibility of overcoming alienation, which he associates with capitalist society. In *Reason and Revolution*, his book devoted to a Hegelian politics, Marcuse writes, "the individuals are isolated from and set against each other. They are linked in the commodities they exchange rather than in their persons. Man's alienation from himself is simultaneously an estrangement from his fellow men." Herbert Marcuse, *Reason and Revolution: Hegel and the Rise of Social Theory*, 2nd ed. (New Jersey: Humanities Press, 1983 [1941]), 279. Fighting to eliminate this estrangement from each other is how Marcuse envisions our political struggle. He cannot recognize alienation itself as emancipatory.

22 Louis Althusser, *For Marx*, trans. Ben Brewster (London: Verso, 1969 [1965]), 45.

23 Althusser conceives of the early Marx as a naïve philosopher of
history. As Althusser puts it, "The untenable thesis upheld by
Marx in the *1844 Manuscripts* was that History is the history of
the process of alienation of a Subject, the Generic Essence of
Man alienated in 'alienated labour.'" Louis Althusser, "Lenin
Before Hegel" (1969), in *Lenin and Philosophy and Other Essays*,
trans. Ben Brewster (New York: Monthly Review Press, 1971),
121. After the break, Althusser claims, Marx comes to see history
as the development of specific economic systems in which
subjectivity plays only an ideological role.

24 Georg Lukács, *History and Class Consciousness: Studies in Marxist
Dialectics*, trans. Rodney Livingstone (Cambridge: MIT Press,
1971 [1922]), 135.

25 Many shorthand accounts of the shift in Marx's thinking away
from alienation narrate a turn from alienation to reification. The
problem with this interpretation is that this term (*Verdinglichkeit*
in German) doesn't appear in *Capital*. It is a contribution from
Georg Lukács and not one endemic to Marx himself.

26 Marx points out that from the capitalist's perspective focused on
profit, labor's role in the creation of this profit will be invisible.
He makes this evident in the second volume of *Capital*, where he
states, "The production process appears simply as an unavoidable
middle term, a necessary evil for the purpose of money-making."
Karl Marx, *Capital: A Critique of Political Economy, Volume Two*,
trans. David Fernbach (New York: Penguin, 1978 [1884]),
137. The emphasis of capitalist production can never be on
production itself.

27 Karl Marx, *Capital: A Critique of Political Economy, Volume Three*,
trans. David Fernbach (New York: Penguin, 1981 [1894]), 127.

28 Karl Marx, *Grundrisse*, trans. Martin Nicolaus (New York:
Penguin, 1993 [1857–1858]), 540.

29 Marx's attack on Proudhon in *The Poverty of Philosophy* is
the earliest critique of technocracy. Although Proudhon is
far removed from the contemporary liberal technocrat, he
nonetheless shares the belief that a technical fix will solve
the problems that inhere within capitalist society. Proudhon's
proposal for eliminating the injustice of the capitalist system fails,
as Marx recognizes, to eliminate the source of the inequality
that capitalism produces. The problem with capitalism is not
a technical one, which is why a technical solution is not in the
offing.

30 According to David Hume, we cannot successfully make the
leap from subjective custom to objective connection. This is
what leads him to claim, "*all our reasonings concerning cause and
effect are deriv'd from nothing but custom.*" David Hume, *A Treatise of
Human Nature* (Oxford: Oxford University Press, 2000), 123. Kant
credits Hume's skepticism with pushing him toward making
the fundamental distinction between appearances and things in
themselves, a distinction that functions as the building block for
his critical philosophy. Without this distinction, Kant would be at
pains to distinguish himself from earlier thinkers.

31 Dieter Henrich, *Between Kant and Hegel: Lectures on German Idealism*,
ed. David S. Pacini (Cambridge: Harvard University Press,
2003), 49.

32 When addressing himself to the Kantian antinomies that indicate
contradictory possibilities without any way to decide between
them — one must either accept both or reject both — Hegel
sees the formation of the antinomy itself as the expression of
ontological contradiction. Rather than impugning reason for
falling into antinomies (as Kant does), Hegel grasps the problem
as its own solution, which becomes visible once one translates
the epistemological problem into ontological terms. For Kant,
an ontological contradiction is simply impossible. But Hegel

deduces the ontological contradiction from the emergence of an intractable epistemological one. Hegel contends that a genuine irresolvable epistemological contradiction must have its origins in ontology. Being itself must be contradictory if it is possible for contradictions such as the Kantian antinomies to arise in the first place. This solution to the problem of the antinomies leaves them in place.

33 Contra Martin Heidegger, in Marx's view there is no universal anxiety in the face of death. Such anxiety exists only for those caught up in the forced individualism of capitalist society. This leads the early Marx to state, "*Death* seems to be a harsh victory of the species over the *definite* individual and to contradict their unity. But the particular individual is only a *particular species being*, and as such mortal." Marx, *Economic and Philosophic Manuscripts*, 138. Almost exactly one hundred and fifty years later, Marxist theorist Fredric Jameson developed this idea further in *The Political Unconscious*. Jameson contends, "in future societies people will still grow old and die, but the Pascalian wager of Marxism lies elsewhere, namely in the idea that death in a fragmented and individualized society is far more frightening and anxiety-laden than in a genuine community, in which dying is something that happens to the group more intensely than it happens to the individual subject." Fredric Jameson, *The Political Unconscious: Narrative as a Socially Symbolic Act* (London: Routledge, 2002 [1981]), 250. For Jameson, death in the communist future will occasion less existential angst because its sharpness will be dissipated into the genuine community. But both Marx and Jameson leave unanswered the question of why this would lessen the impact of death rather than augmenting it. The problem with this line of thought is that it isn't thought through. Not only is the particular individual mortal, but so is the entire species and everything that will ever live. In this sense, anxiety about one's

individual death acts as a synecdoche for anxiety about the heat death of the universe, which Marx might have recognized.

34 Marx, *Economic and Philosophic Manuscripts*, 135.

35 Marx, *Economic and Philosophic Manuscripts*, 135.

36 Karl Marx, *A Contribution to the Critique of Political Economy*, trans. S. W. Ryazanskaya (New York: International Publishers, 1970 [1859]), 21.

37 Georg Lukács takes this idea to its absolute conclusion when he identifies Kant's antinomies of pure reason as the contradictions that result from the dominance of the capitalist mode of production. The solution to the antinomies, as Lukács sees it, resides not in Hegel's turn from epistemology to ontology but in the political practice of the proletariat. As the subject of history, the proletariat solves these apparently impossible theoretical antinomies, which are nothing but the result of the limitations of bourgeois consciousness. In *History and Class Consciousness*, Lukács contends, "As a result of its incapacity to understand history, the contemplative attitude of the bourgeoisie became polarised into two extremes: on the one hand, there were the 'great individuals' viewed as the autocratic makers of history, on the other hand, there were the 'natural laws' of the historical environment." Lukács, *History and Class Consciousness*, 158. Once we take up the perspective of the proletariat as the subject of history, this antinomy between freedom and determinism that Kant confronts as insoluble simply dissolves. The solution resides in the political practice of the rising class.

38 Marx, *Capital, Volume Three*, 958–959.

39 Ray Kurzweil is a proponent of transhumanism. He thinks that we can evolve out of our subjectivity into a collective and therefore unalienated existence through technology.

Chapter Five

1   Jürgen Habermas, *The Structural Transformation of the Public Sphere: An Inquiry into a Category of Bourgeois Society*, trans. Thomas Burger with Frederick Lawrence (Cambridge: MIT Press, 1989 [1962]), 161.

2   While accepting the importance of the public sphere for the project of emancipation, Nancy Fraser criticizes Habermas's conception of it for its narrowness. She contends that we need multiple public spheres to accommodate the diversity of the cultural groups to be represented. She claims, "public life in egalitarian, multi-cultural societies cannot consist exclusively in a single, comprehensive public sphere. That would be tantamount to filling diverse rhetorical and stylistic norms through a single, overarching lens." Nancy Fraser, "Rethinking the Public Sphere: A Contribution to the Critique of Actually Existing Democracy," *Social Text* 25/26 (1990): 69. Despite her critique of Habermas's singular vision of the public sphere, Fraser retains his notion that we interact in public as private identities. She doesn't see the relationship between the public and alienation from identity.

3   The problem with social media is that it corresponds to the private ownership of the public. Private corporations or individuals take control of the space for public debate and interaction. As this transpires, the alienation that coincides with the public realm becomes less readily apparent. Those participating on social media can do so while clinging to their private identities — or as a way of developing their brands.

4   Or one might say that the public space provides us with a form to inhabit. In *The Order of Forms*, Anna Kornbluh argues for rethinking form as the basis of our sociality. She writes, "Formalization as ideal gives us to think the formal state, the forms of sociality that underscore their own antagonistic character." Anna Kornbluh, *The Order of Forms: Realism, Formalism,*

and Social Space (Chicago: University of Chicago Press, 2019), 154.
Form structures a public without the exclusions that community
requires. According to Kornbluh, form provides the basis for any
possible collective existence by highlighting rather than repressing
contradiction. When we turn away from it, we lose the possibility
of seeing connection through our shared alienation.

5   Søren Kierkegaard resists Christianity becoming a community
because he wants to preserve the problem of alienated
subjectivity. This position is the reason why most people rightfully
consider him the parent figure of existentialism. For Kierkegaard,
the name *Christendom* signifies the form that Christianity takes
when it becomes a community, a development that he denounces
at every turn. He opposes the subject that has faith to the person
who adopts a Christian identity within the community and
thereby tries to escape the questions of existence. As he sees it,
Christianity should make these questions more pressing rather
than providing relief from them.

6   Slavoj Žižek is the great theorist of the significance of unwritten
rules for holding a community together. He recognizes that
unwritten rules are necessary for creating the community
bond because they enable the members of the community to
distinguish between those who really belong and those who
are feigning an investment in it. In *The Metastases of Enjoyment*,
he writes, "Explicit, public rules do not suffice, so they have to
be supplemented by a clandestine 'unwritten' code aimed at
those who, although they violate no public rules, maintain a
kind of inner distance and do not truly identify with the 'spirit
of community.'" Slavoj Žižek, *The Metastases of Enjoyment: Six
Essays on Woman and Causality* (London: Verso, 1994), 55. Žižek
goes on to add that the unwritten rules are not just distinct from
the public rules but must contradict them. Obedience to the
unwritten rules necessitates disobedience of the public ones.

7   This was a very low bar on my college team, which was the
    Earlham College Quakers. The team was so consistently
    inept that approximately thirty years after my graduation, the
    school disbanded it. The team's lack of success culminated
    in a collegiate football record for longest losing streak, which
    precipitated the college's decision to finally put an end to things.

8   The community and the team were not identical because it
    was possible to be on a team but not part of the community
    surrounding it, which was the case for certain players.

9   Even the favorite gesture of the contemporary liberal white
    subject — pointing out white privilege — doesn't avow whiteness
    as a community. Instead, it has the opposite effect. The invocation
    of white privilege creates the impression for oneself and others
    that whiteness is not a community at all, which is why it has a
    privilege attached to it. Everyone else submits to the dictates of a
    community, but whites imagine themselves above the fray. This is
    the privilege that they refer to.

10 Because whiteness isn't enough to show that one belongs to the
    white community, it is possible for those who are white to reject
    their adherence to this community. This involves refusing to obey
    the implicit demands that it issues. One can always betray one's
    community as a result of one's alienation from every symbolic
    identity.

11 One form of antiracist activism involves highlighting whiteness
    as a community rather than allowing it to sustain the appearance
    of neutrality that obfuscates its status as a community. When a
    community operates in the dark (as whiteness tends to do), it has
    much more power over subjects than communities functioning in
    the open.

12 Another term for the public is the *commons*, a word that
    increasingly crops up in contemporary thinking. While some
    theorists associate the commons with community because of the

words' shared linguistic roots, there is a fundamental distinction between them to be made. The commons does not promise belonging in the way that community does.

13   In *Civilization and Its Discontents*, Freud claims that there is a fundamental antagonism between the social order and the individual subject, even in societies more focused on the collective than the contemporary liberal one. He states, "A good part of the struggles of mankind centre round the single task of finding an expedient accommodation — one, that is, that will bring happiness — between this claim of the individual [to individual liberty] and the cultural claims of the group; and one of the problems that touches the fate of humanity is whether such an accommodation can be reached by means of some particular form of civilization or whether this conflict is irreconcilable." Sigmund Freud, *Civilization and Its Discontents*, trans. James Strachey, in *The Standard Edition of the Complete Psychological Works of Sigmund Freud*, ed. James Strachey, vol. 21 (London: Hogarth, 1961 [1930]), 96. Even though Freud here leaves the possible resolution of this conflict as an open question, he writes the entire book to show that no resolution is imaginable. No matter what political changes we bring about, the antagonism between society and the subject will endure.

14   Even worse, Clinton gave a signifier to conservative groups that should properly be a signifier of emancipation. A "basket of deplorables" should signify those who come together in their nonbelonging. It should not be the property of those who assert their belonging through the ostracism of Jews, immigrants, and others.

15   I was one of the idiots who held this position, at least in the past. When I would vehemently denounce gated communities, I would proclaim that the gate obviated the community, not recognizing that it constituted it.

16 When my spouse and I were moving to Los Angeles, we consulted an acquaintance who had lived there. She provided information about nice spots to eat, the best movie theaters, and recommended the Hollywood Bowl for musical events. All great suggestions, especially the Hollywood Bowl, where one could see a performance of Beethoven's Ninth Symphony for $1 per ticket. However, she also warned us against taking the bus, claiming that the inexpensive fare resulted in a situation where "anyone can ride." For her, it was the public nature of the bus that made it a site of danger to her (and potentially our) subjectivity.

17 Although Rosa Parks is an icon of the civil rights movement for her refusal to give up her seat, Claudette Colvin refused to give up her seat on a public bus in Montgomery months before Parks. As an unmarried pregnant teenager, Colvin did not appear, in the eyes of Black leaders, to be a good representative for the movement. As a result, Parks became known as the first to refuse to give up her seat even though Colvin preceded her.

18 Hannah Arendt vigorously defends the public against the private assaults on it that occur in modernity. But according to Arendt, the public is not alien. It has a world in which people are at home, a world to which they can belong. In *The Human Condition*, the problem of constituting the public is a problem of overcoming alienation, not accepting it. She writes, "World alienation, and not self-alienation as Marx thought, has been the hallmark of the modern age." Hannah Arendt, *The Human Condition*, 2nd ed. (Chicago: University of Chicago Press, 1998 [1958]), 254. To diagnose the problem of world alienation in this way is to argue for its overcoming. Despite Arendt's concern for the public realm, she doesn't see that it must be alienating to be properly public. To attempt to overcome alienation is always to enter the domain of privacy.

19 In *Cosmopolitanism*, Kwame Anthony Appiah modifies humanism
    to account for cultural difference. In doing so, he accepts that
    there can be no assurance of agreement about what our universal
    values are. He writes, "Cosmopolitans suppose that all cultures
    have enough overlap in their vocabulary of values to begin a
    conversation. But they don't suppose, like some universalists,
    that we could all come to agreement if only we had the same
    vocabulary." Kwame Anthony Appiah, *Cosmopolitanism: Ethics
    in a World of Strangers* (New York: Norton, 2006), 57. Unlike the
    humanist who believes in shared human values, Appiah believes
    only in a common capacity for discussion about these values.

20 John Locke, *Two Treatises of Government* (Cambridge: Cambridge
    University Press, 1988 [1689]), 283.

21 This is a point that Charles Mills insists on in *The Racial Contract*.
    The human becomes human only through the exclusion of those
    considered nonhuman and in need of humanizing.

22 Juliet McMaster, *Jane Austen the Novelist: Essays Past and Present* (New
    York: St Martin's Press, 1996), 16. If Austen's universe is one of
    moral order, the inhabitants of that universe are often exemplars
    of virtue. Alasdair MacIntyre claims that Austen is "the last great
    representative of the classical tradition of the virtues." Alasdair
    MacIntyre, *After Virtue: A Study in Moral Theory* (South Bend:
    University of Notre Dame Press, 1981), 226. For someone like
    MacIntyre, we read Austen's novels looking for moral figures to
    emulate. We read to discover path toward becoming virtuous.

23 Robyn Warhol, "The Look, the Body, and the Heroine: A
    Feminist-Narratological Reading of *Persuasion*," *Novel: A Forum on
    Fiction* 26.1 (1992): 5.

24 According to Byung-Chul Han, not only does direct exposure
    impede love, it also turns every relation into a pornographic one.
    In *The Transparency Society*, he says, "Precisely where the secret
    vanishes in favor of total exhibition and bareness, pornography

begins. It is characterized by penetrating, intrusive positivity." Byung-Chul Han, *The Transparency Society*, trans. Erik Butler (Stanford: Stanford University Press, 2015 [2012]), 26. Austen's novels show what is lost when the reign of privacy prevails.

25   While it may have other virtues, the more recent film version of *Persuasion* (Carrie Cracknell, 2022) does not opt to focus on the significance of public alienation in the way that the earlier film version does.

26   Anne Elliot is the quietest of Austen's heroes. While the earlier novels illustrate the necessity of a misunderstanding that the public realm produces, none show to the extent that *Persuasion* does the burden of alienation that accompanies this realm. Anne's silence speaks her alienation, which only Wentworth can hear.

27   The film leads us to think, if only the parade didn't go by at this moment, we could hear what Anne and Captain Wentworth really feel for each other. But here the external event is working to hide the fact that such a direct communication is impossible. If we were to witness a direct communication between Anne and Captain Wentworth, this would reduce their love to a commonplace affair. Only insofar as it remains uncommunicated can we continue to believe in the truth of their love. The external hindrances are there simply to disguise this fact, as is revealed when, in the final scene of the film (when they are together on a ship), Anne and Captain Wentworth still do not speak.

28   If we examine the ways in which Michell's film deviates from Austen's novel (and this scene is one of the few instances of such deviation), we can see even more pointedly the film's concern with thematizing the public. Michell changes or creates three scenes toward the end of the film: he adds the noisy parade at the point when Anne and Wentworth reveal their love for each other; he alters the penultimate party scene by withholding

knowledge from the audience and by having Wentworth use the occasion to announce the engagement; and he includes a final scene with Anne and Wentworth together on a navy ship (looking at each other, still without speaking). Because these three deviations from the novel have the effect of making even more present the uncertainty and obfuscations of a public world, they provide a further indication that the public world and its requisite alienation are the central preoccupation of Michell's *Persuasion*.

29   The proliferation of private interests in the public world has the effect of destroying it as an inhabitable, neutral space, forcing everyone to live in their own private world without reprieve. In *Read My Desire*, Joan Copjec points out that the contemporary retreat into privacy brings about "the destruction of the *civitas* itself, of increasingly larger portions of our public space. We no longer attempt to safeguard the empty 'private' space… but to dwell within this space *exclusively*." Joan Copjec, *Read My Desire: Lacan Against the Historicists* (Cambridge: MIT Press, 1994), 183. The problem is that the destruction of the public world doesn't represent a liberation into privacy. Instead, it makes our private worlds visible. As the public world disappears, we lose the distance between public and private which allowed the private world to be a respite from the public one.

30   The German language illustrates the connection between the public and its constitutive openness. The word for open in German, *offen*, corresponds, with the addition of an umlaut, to the word for the public, *Öffentlichkeit*. The public is derived from its openness, even linguistically, at least in this case.

31   The euphemism that refers to the homeless as *houseless* or *unhoused* represents an effort to obscure the fact that public space in capitalist society cannot serve as a home. It is a supreme ideological gesture, one that enables people employing the term to feel better about those designated by it while doing nothing at all to change their actual situation.

32 Thinking of private space as primary and public space as secondary is akin to considering the natural state of humanity as one of innocence that is subsequently lost with a fall into sin. Like the image of the Garden of Eden, privacy enables us to imagine ourselves self-identical, whereas in public, our alienation confronts us at every turn.

33 For many champions of the public, or the commons, it is appealing because it marks the point at which we overcome our alienated private identities. What this position misses is that the public doesn't offer relief from alienation but doubles down on it. Private identities are appealing because they lead us to believe we can escape the alienating public realm. For a popular instance of this conception of the public, see Michael Hardt and Antonio Negri, *Commonwealth* (Cambridge: Harvard University Press, 2009).

Conclusion

1 Bertolt Brecht, "The Street Scene," in *Brecht on Theatre*, ed. and trans. John Willett (New York: Hill and Wang, 1964), 125. Brecht also argues for what he calls an epic theater, a theater that alienates the spectator rather than allowing for their identification with what happens on the stage. In his "Short Description of a New Technique of Acting which Produces an Alienation Effect," he states, "The A-effect consists in turning the object of which one is to be made aware, to which one's attention is to be drawn, from something ordinary familiar, immediately accessible, into something peculiar, striking, and unexpected." Bertolt Brecht, "Short Description of a New Technique of Acting which Produces an Alienation Effect" (1940), *Brecht on Theatre*, ed. and trans. John Willett (New York: Hill and Wang, 1964), 143. While seeming to depart from Marx's position, Brecht's embrace of

alienation occurs only for the sake of educating the spectator
about the alienating conditions that prevail in bourgeois society.

2   Joseph Breuer and Sigmund Freud, *Studies on Hysteria*, trans. James
Strachey, in *The Standard Edition of the Complete Psychological Works of
Sigmund Freud*, ed. James Strachey (London: Hogarth Press, 1955
[1895]), 305.

Acknowledgments

Thanks to *Crisis and Critique* for permission to publish a revised version of part of the essay "A Divided Emancipation: The Alienation of the Modern Tragic Hero" in a section of chapter 2 of this book.

I appreciate Carl Neville for asking me to write something for Repeater and Josh Tuner for shepherding the book through the production process. Thanks to Wyk McGowan for always being present as an absence.

My twin sons, Dashiell and Theo Neroni, never allow me to forget that I don't belong even when I'm at home. I'm grateful for this consideration.

Bea Bookchin has still not convinced me that local autonomy is salutary, but I'm indebted to her for continually trying. Our debates don't make her any less my role model.

Thanks to Anna Kornbluh and Russell Sbriglia for helping me remain ensconced in my private world while thinking through the problem of the public.

I appreciate the support of Clint Burnham, Joan Copjec, Matthew Flisfeder, Sheldon George, Scott Krzych, Don Kunze, Juan Pablo Lucchelli, Hugh Manon, Quentin Martin, Jonathan Mulrooney, Carol Owens, Kenneth Reinhard, Frances Restuccia, Molly Rothenberg, Stephanie Swales, John Waldron, Louis-Paul Willis, Jean Wyatt, Hyon Joo Yoo, and Cindy Zeiher.

Thanks to Sheila Kunkle for always being just distant

enough from where everyone expects her to be. This allows her to grasp what I wish that I saw.

The idea for this book originated on a *Why Theory* podcast that I did with Ryan Engley. Since then, he has constantly surprised me with an insight that dislodged me from whatever comfort I had fallen into.

Slavoj Žižek helps too many people, but I'm grateful that didn't stop before he got to me.

Walter Davis demonstrates how insisting on one's alienation can drive political action. He has always kept alive a certain existentialist spirit, no matter how unpopular it became.

Thanks to Jennifer Friedlander and Henry Krips for helping to organize a few of us in our shared alienation and for living out that alienation themselves.

Richard Boothby has changed everything for me since we ran into each other. When he's at sea, so am I.

Mari Ruti died while I was finishing this book. Much of my inspiration for writing this book went with her.

I'm grateful to Hilary Neroni for correcting the errors that she couldn't live with and leaving the rest.

Daniel Cho convinced me not to publish the book I had initially written. In this way, he made sure that he alone would be aware of how shameful the book was. Hopefully he also made this one less shameful.

Thanks to Walter Davis, Paul Eisenstein, and Hilary Neroni. We're the three best friends that anyone could have.

Repeater Books

is dedicated to the creation of a new reality. The landscape of twenty-first-century arts and letters is faded and inert, riven by fashionable cynicism, egotistical self-reference and a nostalgia for the recent past. Repeater intends to add its voice to those movements that wish to enter history and assert control over its currents, gathering together scattered and isolated voices with those who have already called for an escape from Capitalist Realism. Our desire is to publish in every sphere and genre, combining vigorous dissent and a pragmatic willingness to succeed where messianic abstraction and quiescent co-option have stalled: abstention is not an option: we are alive and we don't agree.